THE NEW TEEN DATING GAME

THE NEW TEEN DATING GAME

▼

Love Dr.

Writers Club Press
San Jose New York Lincoln Shanghai

The New Teen Dating Game

Writers Club Press
an imprint of iUniverse, Inc.

For information address:
iUniverse, Inc.
5220 S. 16th St., Suite 200
Lincoln, NE 68512
www.iuniverse.com

ISBN: 0-595-20994-7

Printed in the United States of America

CONTENTS

▼

FOREWORD

▼

The ultimate goal of dating is to achieve a satisfying, exciting, romantic and sexual relationship which will last and be a cornerstone of your life. The material in this book is meant to be an informative educational guide to help you achieve that goal. The unfortunate fact is that today far too many people find themselves chronically dissatisfied with their relationships and sex lives. The saddest thing about these situations is that in all too many cases the lack of satisfaction does not originate from any fundamental, physical or emotion deficiency, but rather from misconceptions and a lack of real useful information on the subject.

The information in the book Teen Dating Game is accurate and up-to-date and is written in a sensitive, direct and easy to understand style. The mission of the book is to provide accurate information and remove the veil of secrecy and the centuries of myths and false beliefs regarding love, relationships, dating and sex. We must re-educate ourselves regarding what love is and how it relates to the dynamics of dating and meaningful sexual relationships. We need to learn to put aside the preconceived notions and misinformation that has been established by the media.

The book *Teen Dating Game* defines the major components to developing a true, rewarding, loving and exciting relationship along with the topics you should avoid so that you do not harm your relationship or your health.

PREFACE

▼

**Do you know the difference between sex,
love and a true relationship?**

Anyone who entered the dating game after the **1980's** knows that dating
as the quaint American institution with all of the rituals and traditions
died in the '80's. As a result of the '70's sex revolution and woman's Lib,
the dating tradition was replaced by "hanging out", so the X generation
and now the Y generation are not familiar with the Emily Post style of dating and the sweet romance of teen socializing and dating.

Thus, the young adults who venture into the uncharted and terrifying
world of adult dating are filled with anxiety and confusion. After the high
school and college relationships have faded people desire to become
involved in a real relationship. However most are confused because they
do not know how to socialize and lack the skills and techniques to develop
a true relationship. As a result many have turned to alternative ways of
socializing like personal ads, dating services, chat rooms, and dating
phone lines because they aren't sure of their socializing skills and need
advice and crave guidelines.

Everyone knows about love, sex and relationships. Everyone desires love, sex and a good relationship, however **very few understand the techniques, components, and requirements to develop a successful loving relationship**. Teens and young adults could use help in managing their sexual relationships, the material in this book is meant to be an informative educational guide to help you achieve that goal. If you have a non-existent love life and crave a rewarding relationship this book can help you fulfill your desires and accomplish your goals.

The ultimate goal of dating is to achieve a satisfying, exciting, romantic and sexual relationship that will last and be a cornerstone of your life. The unfortunate fact is that today far too many people find themselves chronically dissatisfied with their relationships and sex lives. The saddest thing about these situations is that in all too many cases the lack of satisfaction does not originate from any fundamental, physical or emotion deficiency, but rather from misconceptions and a lack of real useful information on the subject.

The information in this book, The New Dating Game, is accurate and up-to-date and is written in a sensitive, direct and easy to understand style. The mission of the book is to provide accurate information and remove the veil of secrecy and the centuries of myths and false beliefs regarding love, relationships, dating and sex. We must reeducate ourselves regarding what love is and how it relates to the dynamics of dating and meaningful sexual relationships. We need to learn to put aside the preconceived notions and misinformation that has been established by the media.

Life is an emotional journey…

…Rescue 911 series can help prepare you and your loved ones for the physical and psychological adventures on that journey!

INTRODUCTION

▼

The Great Lover Series of books is a collection of information committed to helping individuals make sound, healthy choices regarding their love lives and sexual activities. This book deals with how teens and young adults can constructively talk about their sexuality and dating. The material reveals the skills and techniques of socializing and dating, and examines and explains some of the various complexities involved in dating like abstinence, safe sex, and the basic fundamentals needed to develop a good relationship.

In order to promote a healthy attitude and responsibility, it's essential to maintain an open, communicative attitude about the topic of sex. This book tackles the tough issues regarding sexuality in a respectful but unblinking manner. The human sexual anatomy is discussed at length in a clear, unambiguous fashion. In addition to explaining the biological ticks of the sexual relationship, we discuss some of the psychological ones as well. We give techniques for broaching the topics of safe sex and abstinence. We discuss how dating can be an even more enjoyable experience without the pressures and dangers involved with having sex. We delve deeply into the subject of sexually transmitted diseases, frankly discussing how these ailments are contracted, their symptoms and treatments, as well as who is really at risk. We explain how much protection safe sex actually is and how to properly utilize it.

This may sound like a lot of information to understand, but keep in mind, that this knowledge will benefit both you and your loved ones throughout your lifetimes. Despite the prevalence of sex in our media and culture, many people remain ignorant about fundamental aspects of the sexual relationship or are confused by conflicting reports and information. It's time to finally distinguish the facts from the fiction. An intelligent, open attitude towards sexuality is vital not only for our own happiness, but for that of our children as well. In order to gain the happiness you desire in life, you must develop the proper behavior and thinking patterns that will produce the conditions you desire in an enjoyable and rewarding sexual relationship.

CHAPTER I

▼

IT'S YOUR FUTURE HAPPINESS

Teenagers face a difficult battle. A surge of emotions, peer pressures, and hormones tells them to rush into becoming sexually active. This drive is in exact opposition to what these same teenagers are told by their parents, religion or moral code. The teen years can be a tough and dangerous time. Teens go through an emotional struggle—their heart and desires verses their conscious. Decisions made with an immature mindset can spell catastrophe later on in life. In order to make the right decisions it's essential to be honest with one's self and to try to keep an open mind.

When growing up, it is important for teens to seek the acceptance and approval of the adults in their life by adopting their likes and dislikes. However, as they grow it may become difficult to separate their beliefs and values from their parents and friends.

Teens or young adults may feel that in order to accepted and liked they have to suppress their own emotions and feelings so that they do not upset others. Many girls will become involved in a controlling relationship because they are willing to sacrifice their true feelings and endure the anxiety they experience in order to be accepted by the one they love and their friends.

Young people may be ruled by fear that they are not attractive enough, smart enough, talented enough, or important enough for others to accept what they feel and say. It is this emotion that causes many teens to get involved with addictions, self-abuse and self-pity.

These mixed emotions can cause a lot of hurting on the emotional journey of life. We want to be happy so much that it is difficult for us to learn to trust our emotions, instincts, desires, wants and needs because no matter where they turn, either the media or others will try to install their beliefs and values in their life.

What young people need to know is that everyone has the same problem especially when it is involving relationships and sex. Everyone wants to have a good relationship and a good sex life, however, very few can talk about it because they feel awkward and it is difficult to be intimate about their feelings.

Millions of Americans find it hard to talk about relationships and sex. Surveys conducted by researchers and institutes strongly support this theory.

Surveys reveal that nearly 9 in 10 men in relationships with women reported serious problems articulating their needs and desires. Nearly half of the women in heterosexual relationships have difficulties articulating their needs and desires when talking to their partners about the relationship or sex. These findings represent all age categories, from teens to seniors.

The surveys reveal that unless people develop the skills to understand then communicate and then cope with the anxiety involved with a relationship and sex, they will continue to have difficulty in resolving problems in their relationships.

It is easier for some to talk about their feelings, however, everyone can learn to overcome their shortcomings and talk intelligently about their feelings and desires. Talking about your needs and sex is doable, you do not need to feel guilty, ashamed, or embarrassed when talking in detail about personal feelings and relationships.

Parents need to be open concerning the topic of sex whether their teens are sexually active or not. Love, sex and relationships can be perilous undertakings for the inexperienced. The information in this book is designed to enable parents and young adults to be able to communicate about the topics that are really important to them. It is possible to protect yourself and your loved ones from AIDS and other STDs, unplanned pregnancies and emotional and physical violence. It all starts with pulling back the veil of secrecy so many people in our society are denied valid and honest information regarding the topic of sex and relationships and the opportunity of simply discussing the topics in an honest and non-critical manner.

Why is it so important to be completely open regarding sexuality? The answer is that unfortunately, all teens are significantly at risk. No matter how good a person is, one misguided or careless sexual encounter can create any number of disastrous results. Saying, "It won't happen to my child," doesn't make it so.

In today's world it has become more difficult for people to become properly prepared for the sexual and emotional journey that they are going to undertake during their lifetime. When people are young they are naturally very involved exploring and defining their own identities while at the same time trying to assert their independence for the first time. Although this is a normal evolutionary process for teenagers, it often creates power struggles and tensions in the parent / child relationship. Unfortunately, no matter how thoughtful a parent is, it is very difficult at times to communicate effectively and to have the child benefit from the parent's experiences and knowledge.

Our young people are especially vulnerable emotionally and physically to the aftermath of an unprepared or premature sexual encounter. Many teenagers are not properly protected against undesired pregnancies, disease and exploitation.

One of the main hurdles for parents to overcome in trying to communicate with their teens is the attitude that, "This doesn't happen to me and my friends, we're above this, that's only what you see on TV." Sadly, most people learn too soon in life that terrible things do happen to every one, from all classes, all economic and educational backgrounds. No matter where you live or work, you and your teenagers are exposed to tremendous temptations, exploitations and risks.

Both for teenagers and young adults, the consequences of indiscriminate, early sexual encounters leaves them exposed to tremendous sexual torment, anxiety and violence unprepared and unplanned pregnancies and the life threatening sexually transmitted diseases.

Although tempting, trying to "turn off" the world is not a viable option. Sometimes parents can become overprotective and shelter their teens too much. Although this may prove to be a solution for a few years, this tactic can ultimately have deeply negative results. Raising teens in a social / sexual vacuum does not prepare them for the real world. When they inevitably have to leave that vacuum, they may find themselves woefully ill equipped to deal with the temptations and pitfalls of adult sexuality.

One of the main major hurdles that parents face with their teens today is addressing the issue of sex in the first place. For generations, centuries really, a veil of secrecy has covered the topic of sexuality and any activity associated with it. As a result, because of cultural backgrounds, religious beliefs and even governmental mandates, we have fostered a system where many people grow up in almost complete ignorance of sex and relationships.

Simply put, the institutions of today's society aren't doing a very good job of teaching the facts. We cannot rely on our schools to impart the proper knowledge and protect our children. Although there are sex education courses given in class, they teach little more than basic anatomy and facts about the birth process. Rarely if ever do they tackle the really tough subjects of sexual activity such as how to establish values, how to build the fundamental elements necessary for a good relationship, what the benefits and drawbacks are of intimacy and pleasure or how to emotionally face that fateful day when a love affair ends. As our society demonstrates constantly, the emotional scars of bad sexual relationships run deep and sometimes never fully heal.

It's a huge mistake to subscribe to the quicksand psychology that if parents and role models preach abstinence and chastity that is all that is necessary. Parents should encourage their children to delay sexual activity, but this doesn't mean that parents should make sexuality a taboo subject. If parents haven't prepared their children, they may be setting them up for calamity latter on. The results of sexual ignorance are just as disastrous for someone at age 23 as they are for someone at 14 or 15. This is clearly shown in the results of numerous research studies, interviews and surveys. Charts or graphs aren't even necessary to prove this point. All most Americans have to do is to look at a weekly magazine or daily newspaper to see the tremendous physical and emotional scars that many bear as a result of terrible sexual relationships. It is not enough to simply postpone going into a relationship. Preparation, information and honesty are needed in order to protect one's self.

At times it seems that too much information has been made available for people to still be irresponsible about sex, and yet it happens constantly. Teenagers have to be made to understand that if someone isn't concerned about their safety regarding a sexual relationship, then they shouldn't enter into one. Only a concerned, intelligent, caring person will insist on safe sex . Self -respect is a slippery topic in regards to teens, and all too often it's determined largely by the view of their peer group. Teens need to be taught that in order for others to respect you, you must respect yourself first. Teenagers need to make it a matter of personal pride that they respect themselves too much to risk their futures or their lives on ill planned, indiscriminate sexual encounters.

In addition, teens must be taught to find a value in people, not in things that people possess. All too often teenagers end up with a twisted perception of affection, equating money, fame or sexual prowess with success in dating and relationships. If left unchecked, such an attitude can form the template of their adult personalities. The real truth is that money, fame and power play a very minor role in a good sexual relationship, and without the right components it's impossible to build a loving, long term connection.

Teens must learn that sex is but a part of a larger experience in life. One of the major factors governing the outcome of a person's life is how they handle their sexual activities. It's essential to always consider the potential life long effects of having sex. There always looms the ominous potential of having an unwanted pregnancy or contracting a painful or even life threatening STD.

No single sex act, no matter how pleasurable, is worth a lifetime of discomfort and pain.

There are thousands of wrong reasons for entering into a sexual relationship. Peer pressure, curiosity, jealousy, trying to impress someone, trying to prove maturity are among the most common. One of the most prevalent and saddest reasons that teens have sex is to feel love, or to attempt to make others love them. However, the only real reason to have a sexual relationship is when two mature, consenting people that are emotionally, mentally, and physically prepared and have had the time to thoroughly think about what they are doing and feel comfortable about their decisions to have a sexual relationship.

Cardinal Rule

Never confuse sex with love. Having sex does not create love.

The most important decision in your lifetime is choosing the right mate and relationship because it will account for the majority of the happiness or misery that you will experience in your future.

Cardinal Rule

Problems are not solved by having sex.
Sadness and low self-esteem are a cause of sex,
and sex is a cause of sadness and low self-esteem.

It is unfortunate, but sexual relationships can present us with enormous problems. A good relationship can be the most wondrous, beautiful, satisfying, rewarding facet of one's life. A poor or bad sexual relationship can be terrifying, emotionally agonizing and in some cases, deadly. It's vital for parents to learn to be understanding and sensitive and for teenagers not to allow their hormones to run rampant and let the mass media dictate their guidelines and values.

One should never let luck be their co-pilot in a sexual relationship.

Sexual Control

The mission of this book is to provide you with enough knowledge and concern to give you a moral backbone and enable you to make the right decision concerning your sexual activity. In the real world most teens are preoccupied with the idea of dating and sex. Teenagers natural curiosity is fed by a constant barrage of sexually suggestive and explicit messages from the media. Like it or not—sex and sexual activity are a part of our every day life and permeate nearly every layer of our society. Whether you approve or disapprove, understand or don't understand, we are confronted with sexual choices every day of our lives. The media has inundated us with information that causes many confusion and anxiety and ultimately ends up negatively influencing our attitudes and behavior

Despite this proliferation of sexually charged material, our society still remains rather nervous towards the subject. The veil of secrecy about sexuality and sexual relationships remains intact even today, leaving both the young and old on their own to understand and explain sexuality. As a result, dangerous ideas and beliefs have been passed on from generation to generation for decades, perhaps even centuries. People learn more regarding sex and sexual activity from uninformed peers and the advertising media than they do from their parents, school or church. In today's society we are experiencing so many poor, bad or failed relationships and an increase in sexually transmitted diseases because people have come to accept and believe these myths.

CHAPTER II

▼

THE NEW PATHWAY

Why Teens and Parents Must Communicate

Before we can discuss such things as abstinence, safe sex and sexual health we need to explain why it is important for parents and teens to communicate, along with providing techniques that promote trust and parent / child closeness.

Few teenagers are mature or emotionally conditioned enough to make them capable of safely managing their sex lives. Therefore responsible and knowledgeable parents need to do whatever is necessary to help guide their teenagers. This is easier said than done, as many parents often need to come to terms with the fact that their teens need their help in the first place.

All teenagers are looking for answers of one sort or another. Many times they are left to draw upon their own experiences and peers to get answers on sex and safe sex. This is an extremely dangerous route because frequently the answers they get are not complete or are just blatantly incorrect. Parents need to be ready to answer their children's questions in a straight forward manner and *not put it off.*. Otherwise they will get the answers from somebody else who might provide bad information or mess with their emotions or morals.

Most generation-Xers discover that hanging out with high school and college pals won't prepare them for the world of no-rules sex and romance.

A free flow of communication is essential to create a solid bond between parents and their teens. Everything that is discussed in this book and all of the information offered will be useless unless one is able to discuss their feelings and thoughts honestly. It's not enough just to speak honestly however. In order to truly succeed as a great communicator one must make their ears honest as well. It's essential for parents to always realize that communication is a two way street, and that stopping to listen often can be more effective than any advice or platitudes that one has to offer.

Cardinal Rule

> **Preventive maintenance is necessary
> to help teenagers through difficult times.**
> **Parents must learn to converse easily with their teens in order to
> help them understand the dangers of being sexually active. Most
> teens really want the help and assurance, but are too nervous or
> embarrassed to ask. Learning to talk about sex with your daughter
> or son can be hard, but it has never been more important.**

Learn to Communicate Honestly

Sometimes the truth hurts, but there are ways to improve your sex-talk skills without hurting the other person or causing bad feelings. You never want to clause an argument because that will only lead to more anxiety and arguments.

The following are simple ways to improve your relationship talk skills:

1. Never leave your sexual wishes and desires to guesswork, learn to communicate them clearly and honestly.

2. Talk to your partner as you would your best friend, learn to confine your real feelings like you would to a friend.

3. When you ask a question, give your partner a chance to answer.

4. Always listen to what he or she is saying with an open mind and be realistic about your decisions. If you cannot agree about something, then try to find a middle ground. Learning to compromise is the secret to eliminating frustration and building a good relationship.

5. If your partner is doing something that pleases you then tell him or her. This is called positive reinforcement. And when a person learns that they are pleasing another person their ego is increased and they will want to please you in the future again and again.

6. Make specific concrete request, such as, "please kiss me, hug me, hold me". A request will more likely give you the desired result then when you express a vague wish like, let's be more romantic".

7. Talk honestly and intimately about sex afterwards, about what he or she did that pleased you, always state your preferences in a positive manner, this will get much better results because you will reinforce a positive feeling. For example, "I like it when you touch me like this" or "I like it when you do this to me", this sounds much better and will get the response you want. When you say something like "you don't do this right, or I don't' like this", you will evoke a hurt feeling and will not get the results that you desire.

8. Never ask your partner to do something that they are not emotionally or mentally capable of doing.

9. Do not ask a question that does not have a realistic or practical answer.

10. Take turns talking about topics that the other person is interested in.

11. Do not get into heated arguments regarding topics that cannot be resolved, like religion, family, politics, careers, or desires this will only evoke long-term anxiety and hurt feelings.

12. Learn to listen to the other person with respect and empathy for their feelings and viewpoints. You may not agree with them, but you do need to understand why they feel the way they do.

13. Learn to laugh at small problems, small faults, minor mistakes, treat your partner like you would your best friend and forgive or overlook innocent mistakes or faults.

14. Never put pressure on your partner to make a decision that they're not ready to make. This could cause resentment or an argument.

15. Be optimistic when your partner is trying to explain something it will make understanding and if necessary forgiving much easier.

16. Remember that many kinds of questions have no right or wrong answer, and no "yes" or "no" answer.

17. Patience and cooperation are necessary to finding the solution to a problem, because sometimes the solution is not obvious or simple and many times there is no quick fix.

18. In order for your relationship to have staying power you must realize, you will never always have the same likes and dislikes. Therefore be honest in expressing your feelings so that the other person does not misunderstand and have a false impression of what you like or don't like. Candor is the key to expressing your likes and dislikes.

19. Don't belittle your partner's wants or desires, learn to show compassion.

20. Learn to establish ground rules regarding the sensitive topics that you will discuss with your partner.

21. When you're wrong learn to say "I'm sorry" sincerely. Do not create a dispute because you cannot say "I'm sorry".

22. Learn to express your feelings by saying, "I love you" and "I care about you". Everyone needs to hear this to reinforce the relationship.

23. Never judge a person based on their actions only, always find out the reason or logic behind the action.

24. Speak with respect to your partner otherwise they may feel threatened and resent talking to you.

25. Whenever someone asks you something that is very personal and you don't want to answer the question, asked them why they need to know? Their reason may help you with your answer.

26. Never verbally attack your mate because they will be unwilling to open up about themselves and may resent what your saying. If they are doing something that annoys you and you want to change their behavior make a positive suggestion of how they could improve the relationship.

27. If you have a pessimistic outlook regarding what your mate is telling you then the conversation will become destined to have a self-fulfilling negative outcome.

28. Do not repudiate another person's values without understanding their feelings, then try to embrace the difference or find a middle ground to compromise.

29. Remember when you're angry that silence may be the best form of communication.

30. If you have a quarrel with your partner try not to involve past events or people, but focus on solving the present issues.

31. Learning to understand and compromise is the secret to a long-term relationship.

Falling in love is easy, staying in love and having a good relationship takes effort.

The most important guideline to good communication is to establish some ground rules regarding your discussion. This will enable you to get your point across without trampling your child's or partners feelings under foot in the process. The main areas that should be observed regarding ground rules are as follows:

1. Never argue or belittle the other person in front of friends, family or in public.

2. Learn to discuss problems and tell your true feelings, even if it's easier for you to lie.

3. Have empathy for the other persons feelings and needs. Don't belittle their wants and desires. Don't dismiss their questions or requests (many times parents assume that their teen is already aware of something, when in reality they're not).

4. Try to never fight or argue when you're angry or upset. Emotions will run rampant and feelings will be severely hurt, many times creating a barrier to communication.

5. Establish some quiet time when you can sit down with the other person and discuss their questions and concerns.

6. Keep a regular channel of communication open. Always let them know that you are there to listen.

7. Don't let friends or neighbors set your standards or opinions.

8. If you have difficulty explaining something because it is an emotional topic you should write it in a note and give the note to the other person. This may prevent heated disagreements.

Establishing some ground rules is very important because it enables families to maintain order in their discussions while promoting self-respect in their children. These aren't rules for parents alone to obey, it's essential for teens to adopt them as well. In this way both parent and child can feel confident and safe when dealing with each other.

How to Communicate With Your Teen Regarding Emotions, Chastity, Pregnancy, and STDs

A new approach to safe sex is needed to change the growing trends of unwanted pregnancies, increasing levels of STDs and abortions. It becomes clear that the traditional approach to solving these problems has not been effective. Information is the key—only by learning the truth about safe sex can one control their future.

This book does not discuss the morality of whether or not one should engage in a sexual relationship outside of marriage. That is a question that has to be answered on an individual basis. It's a decision that can't be made lightly. It's essential for one to openly and honestly examine their own moral, cultural and religious values before choosing whether or not to become sexually active. A large part of making that decision is gaining an intelligent understanding of what exactly safe sex is and how it can be implemented in a relationship.

Categories of safe sex:

1. Abstinence and chastity

2. Sexual history and medical exams

3. Safe sex procedures

It's essential that parents explain to their children what they'll need to know when they eventually do enter into a sexual relationship. First and foremost, teens need to be taught to understand STDs, and to realize the need to talk to their potential partner about them *BEFORE* they have any sort of intimate contact. Parents must stress to their teens the importance of being honest with their partners about their own health as well. Telling a prospective partner about one's medical history can be difficult, but it's an important responsibility. Teens need to understand that patience is a virtue in relationships. One must allow enough time to get to know their partner before becoming intimate with that person. There are no short cuts for gaining trust. Even if a teen is still years away from sexual activity, it's important for them to understand how to properly communicate about sexual health and medical histories for when that time inevitably comes.

When Do You Discuss STDs or Medical Histories With Your Partner?

It's essential to broach the topic of medical histories and sexual health before any sort of intimacy happens in a relationship. All too often people wait until they have become engaged in a passionate session to tell their partner about their STD. This is a thoughtless tactic that can very often lead to hurt feelings or a complete break up. It's best for one to stay relaxed and confident and to explain to their partner in a quiet manner what has been involved with their medical history or sexual health.

Even if sexual contact has already occurred, it's still never too late to have this discussion.

Where Do You Want to Talk to Your Partner About Your Medical History or STD?

Any sensitive discussions should occur someplace that is secure, private and safe. It's important for both partners in the relationship to feel as comfortable as possible. It's a mistake to have such a talk in a public place. One should never have this discussion on the phone or over a computer as this is immensely impersonal and likely to cause hurt feelings.

What Do You Confide In Your Partner?

When a person wants to discuss their medical history or sexually transmitted disease with a partner, it always helps to express respect and trust before the discussion even begins. Once the conversation has started, it's important to remain positive and open to questions and concerns. There are certain questions that must be answered before any sexual contact occurs. It's vital to find out if both partners have always used proper protection in prior relationships (such as a condom). Discussing past sex partners is important as well, but is a topic that must be handled sensitively and non-critically.

As many STDs have an incubation period of months, it might not be obviously apparent that a person is infected. Current medical exams and blood work are the only truly reliable ways of determining whether or not an STD is present, so both partners should get a check up if they've been sexually active previously. If an STD is involved in either partner's health profile, it needs to be frankly discussed. Treatments and protective measures need to be determined before the relationship can proceed any further.

It's important to stay positive. Getting involved with issues of blame, guilt or fault finding accomplishes nothing and can only lead to anger or depression. Talking about sexual health can be uncomfortable at first, but it ultimately creates more trust and intimacy in a relationship when handled in a thoughtful manner.

It takes only one unprotected encounter to contract a sexually transmitted disease. No single sex act is worth a lifetime of discomfort or your life itself. Always be concerned enough to ask about a partner's medical history.

Cardinal Rule

A loving relationship is a two-way street. **Remember no one is without fault. Understanding and compromise is the key to unlocking happiness.**

A sexual relationship is as much an emotional state of mind as a physical relationship. The thoughts of another, the anticipation of an affair, the planning of a romantic interlude, a loving, note, a caring whisper in the ear, a special look or gesture, a phone call, a thoughtful act, words of praise or encouragement, a hug, a tender touch, sharing a special moment together, having that someone special near you, words of understanding, a helping hand, trust, loyalty, are all part of a good sexual relationship, and may bring the greatest pleasures and create the strongest bond, if done at the proper time and when you are prepared.

In order to establish a good sexual relationship, both parties must be emotionally mature and emotionally prepared and have a good attitude toward sex. Without these key elements no physical stimulation, no physical enticements will ever result in achieving a truly wonderful, satisfying and pleasurable sexual relationship by themselves. It is only in concert with one's mental and emotional state that one can truly experience the ultimate sexual relationship.

Thus the key to developing a good sexual relationship is to have good communication between the partners and to make sure that they are both emotionally prepared to develop a pleasurable and satisfying sexual relationship. Without this mutual understanding and consent the relationship will never be able to obtain its full goals and develop a sound foundation for a caring long term, relationship.

The first major step in developing a good sexual relationship is to understand you cannot control the relationship. You cannot control another's feelings. You may try, however, history shows that this never succeeds in the long run. Trying to control the other individual's feelings many times will push that person away from you and destroy whatever feelings you have for each other. The two key things is developing a good sexual relationship is understanding and using the key elements of a sexual relationship and consent by the individuals. Therefore, in developing a good relationship you must learn to adjust and understand. You must have empathy for the other person's feelings and needs. Find out what will make them fulfilled and happy, then incorporate these elements into your relationships. A relationship is a unique bond between two individuals that is held together by intimacy and honesty. The intimacy and honesty that creates the unity of a relationship.

The intimacy and honesty allows people to become closer and closer until that bond enables the person to not only grow within themselves, but support and help the other person grow in the relationship as well. Honest communication is the key to developing a good relationship; it is the key to understanding chastity. Honestly expressing yourself is the key to control STD's and it is the major component which you have control over in a relationship. Without honest communication you will never establish trust in your relationship. Honesty and trust are the cornerstones of a solid relationship. Without trust in a relationship you will never be able to discuss and practice chastity, abstinence and safe sex.

CHAPTER III

▼

THE ART OF DATING
AND SOCIALIZING

Developing a relationship is hard work, it takes time, negotiation, compromises, and energy. This helpful guide offers advice, tips and techniques to help you deal with the anxieties and uncertainties incurred with socializing and the first steps of dating.

1. When you first meet someone say hello with enthusiasm put some energy and sparkle in your voice do not project anxiety or nervousness.

2. Reach out and shake hands in a sensitive and polite manner, if the occasion allows give the person a welcome hug. How you touch a person will give the signal if you are interested.

3. Make eye contact. Eye contact establishes intimacy, and coordinate eye contact with what you are saying. Timing with eye contact can convey intent and emotion between people.

4. When introduced remind the person of your name and repeat their name, this shows interest on your part.

5. To start the conversation, ask the person a question about themselves. People are usually interested in talking about themselves, in fact the way to start relationships is by showing interest in what the other person is saying. Showing interest in what the other person is saying will flatter the other person's ego.

6. When the opportunity happens, agree with or confirm the other person's viewpoint. One of the facets of love is when the other person feels that you affirm the view of what they like to think they are.

7. Ask the person something personal or something about their past. People like to talk about themselves and after they reveal some of their inner feelings, thoughts and ambitions, they will feel closer to you. However, the key is to ask questions in a natural manner so that should not put them on the defense and cause anxiety.

8. Try to find common areas of interests. The easiest, fastest, and best way to develop a friendship is to share thoughts about a common interest. Try to keep up to date and familiarize yourself with current happenings like records, videos, movies, books, events, and news of the day.

9. Once you have achieved a friendship, usually events and nature will guide and develop the relationship along. However, keep in mind, do not depend on others to make things happen, you need to start things in motion, do not monopolize the conversation or any viewpoint. This can be a real turn off. Do not fidget, this may annoy, the other person and cause them to have anxiety. Do not play games or lie,—this can destroy a friendship very quickly.

10. It is important in the beginning of a relationship to keep you eyes and your heart open and to extend trust to your new partner. Never

start a relationship by comparing your new partner to a prior relationship or by requiring the new partner to "prove themselves in
advance" because of past problems with other relationships.

 *   Make up your mind to be happy and pleasant-people enjoy
      being around people who are happy.

Cardinal Rule

> **If you have a pessimistic outlook regarding trust you
> will become destined to have a negative self-fulfilling prophecy.**

Once a person is disappointed, it is difficult to find the courage to trust
again. However, it is a key element in developing a good sexual relationship. You must have a firm foundation because honesty and trust are one
of the cornerstones of a solid relationship. You must be able to give the
opportunity to the new partner that you trust them and that you are honest with them and allow them to express their trust in you and be honest
with you. Only in this way will you be able to work on the other steps and
elements in a relationship. Without trust and honesty you will never truly
attain true intimacy in a relationship.

  * In a relationship, it is very important to make your partner your best
friend. When you are not feeling well, when you have moods, when you
have desires, confide in your partner. Let them know your different sides
of your personality. This way they can become closer and more intimate.

Cardinal Rule

> **Everything is nicer when shared with a special friend.**

You can establish a good friendship by sharing your past and your present happenings, telling him or her the likes and dislikes that you have
regarding music, food, sporting events, being able to laugh at yourself and

at your partner, sharing goofy times as well as serous times. Learn to never take yourself or your partner too seriously. When little or unimportant things happen, be able to see the lighter side or the humor in something. If someone spills something, for example, and your partner's embarrassed, learn to see the humor in it. Have them relax. It's just a passing moment. Learn to comfort your partner just like you would your best friend. Learn how to confide your deepest feelings to your partner. And always learn to be there for the other person.

Keep in mind that you do not want to exert extreme pressure on your partner to do things that are not within their comfort levels. Compromising is about feeling comfortable and secure by both parties, not having everything your way, or that the other person must constantly prove their devotion by always giving in. Keep these things in mind when you have your problems and they will help to guide you through to a good solution.

* It is better to say you are sorry than to be sorry you did not say it. All relationships will have times when there is conflict and people will fight. It is how you handle the conflict that is important, more important many times than what you are actually arguing or disagreeing about. Because over a period of time, people have a tendency to forget what they were fighting about, but they remember the harsh words or the results of a fight or argument. So it is important to not distort the facts, make generalizations, pull in prior events or relationships, or belittle the other person and their viewpoint or comments. You must learn to fight fairly, to express your problems and concerns without becoming a dirty fighter. You must be able to express your feelings when you have anger, but do it in a manner that is constructive so that the other person in the relationship has an opportunity to understand and to make amends. You must always allow the opportunity for the other person to apologize and say I'm sorry. And once they have taken that step, you must be in a position to forgive and go on. A **major obstacle** can come about in a relationship when one partner or the other either cannot say **I'm sorry or cannot forgive** and go on. If

you hold this anger and hatred or frustration you are destined to create a feud and there will never be a satisfactory end. You will take that anger, disappointment or hatred to the grave with you.

When your mate attacks you verbally, the natural reaction is to defend yourself, however, a neutral statement or I'm sorry can diffuse the other person and prevent an argument. For example: A woman is upset and yells at her man that he never takes out the trash or helps with watching the children. The man feels attached and responds, "That's your job" or "Don't bother me." Now the woman feels angry and needs to make a comeback—and then the argument escalates. A good response would be if he says, "I'm sorry, I'll try to do better" or "You're right, I'll try to help more". The argument is diffused and the woman's anxiety is released.

One of the major elements of a long-term relationship is the ability to go on with the relationship, to find a solution, to compromise or to work out the problem and to forgive and be able to have the quality to under-stand and apologize. Without this, you never are truly in a relationship where you can kiss and make up.

Cardinal Rule

A good relationship is a two-way street remember.
No one is without fault.
Compromise is the key to unlock happiness.

* We all find it appealing to be involved with a partner who can show affection. You must let yourself be free and comfortable. Be able to show affection. Give a little snuggle. Hold a hand at the right time. A little kiss on the cheek. A caress, a pat, a touch. Sometimes even playfully wrestle or hug your partner. Or come up behind them and give then a surprise hug. Leaving little notes for someone, or a flower, or a surprise gift. Or mailing them a card. And especially being able to keep in touch with the someone special. Give then a call at work or home, if for nothing more than to say

I miss you, I'm thinking about you, I need you, I love you. This can really make people feel exhilarated and happy and add a little sunshine to everyone's day.

Cardinal Rule

Put humor in your daily life, make time to do fun things together.

* Appearance is usually the first thing that attracts one person to another. However, it is usually also the weakest link in keeping two people together in a long-term relationship.

Do not confuse appearance with style or wealth. Style is usually someone else's perception of what looks good and may not necessarily be attractive for you. And secondly, many people confuse expensive items with good appearance. It is just as easy for someone to look attractive and have good appearance on a very modest budget, as it is for someone with a lot of money to buy expensive things that look awkward and even unattractive.

Many people in our society are influence by our environment and as a result the clothing we wear is a reflection of that environment. There are two common mistakes that most people make when planning a wardrobe and deciding what to wear. First, they let fashion designer's dictate what they should wear. Many times this apparel will not compliment the person's physical makeup or coloring, and in the case of accessories like women's shoes, may even cause physical discomfort and harm. Second, we allow our peers to influence our choice of dress rather than picking out what suits our particular needs.

For example, think back twenty years ago or so, would the high school and college students of that date even consider wearing woman's coveralls, pants that were three sizes too big, or wear shirts or sweatshirts so big that they would hang down over their knees. Twenty years ago people would run screaming at the thought of wearing such articles. Yet today on the high school and college campuses across the nation this is considered "in fashion". The fact that also proves this is that the same young adults will pay substantially higher prices for articles that have a certain logo or brand name, although the quality of the garment leaves a lot to be desired.

Designers need to feed both their pocketbooks and their egos and therefore they are under pressure to meet seasonal demands to change the style of something and to make it chic. Although designers over the years have been responsible at times for some very positive changes in apparel, most of the changes usually are not flattering and are short lived. We have to be able to focus on what is truly good quality, and what makes you, the individual, look attractive.

Be honest with yourself, look at your wardrobe and find those things that really look appropriate and attractive on you regardless of what your friends and peers may first say, because the real truth is **our appearance makes a great impact on how we are treated socially**. People who look good and have a nice appearance and look successful receive preferential treatment in almost all levels of social life as well as in the corporate business world. This fact has been proven in many research studies.

The same point has been dramatically proven time and time again by the entertainment and movie industry. The identical woman when she is dressed in something like sweat pants and a pullover versus an appropriate attractive outfit will make people of both genders stop and turn heads. Just look at the covers of almost all your women's magazines and social magazines. You never see the woman dressed in moccasins, sweat pants and a tee shirt.

The key is to be able to pick the appropriate patterns, shades of colors and textures on an inexpensive budget that will accent your appearance and will enable you to look attractive and right for all occasions.

There are only basically two reasons to dress. One, to protect yourself from the elements of heat and cold, rain, sleet, sun and secondly to look good for the people you are meeting and to make yourself feel good about yourself. A nice outfit always pumps up one's ego.

Being attractively dressed and well groomed will boost your ego help give you the self-confidence to overcome that nervous tension when you meet somebody new or when you are going to a social function. More importantly, being properly groomed and looking attractive will have a significant effect upon the people you are meeting. Especially if it is that one special person.

However, a world of warning, do not fall into the soap opera type thinking when people on TV make a decision for a relationship based solely on looks and money and do not use sound judgments. You may be setting yourself up for a big letdown, frustration, loneliness, depression, because your life and relationship can end like the ones on TV.

Everyone always notices a nicely groomed person. Appearance is so important because it gives you self-confidence. It shows you care. We are attracted to each other by our appearance. Appearance can start the chemistry between people. It may be a style of hair, the way the person wears the clothes, the certain look or style that they incorporate in their fashion. If advertising firms pay huge fees to have good looking, well groomed people in nice attire stand next to the product to attract attentions, should you do any less when you are trying to attract someone?

CHAPTER IV

▼

ROMANCE AND SEDUCTION

This chapter was developed as a guide for you to understand the components of the emotion of love and to learn the art of romance and seduction in order to help you to achieve the relationship you desire.

Most people think of candlelight, music, flowers, a sunset, or an exotic dinner, when they think of romance and love. However, romance and seduction go much deeper because it involves the chemistry between the people-and their inner feelings. Candlelight, music and perfume will enhance the romantic atmosphere, but it will never replace the true feelings and chemistry between people. This chapter will guide you through the romance and seduction elements that are necessary to get that someone special to react to you in the way you desire.

Cardinal Rule

**Seduction is the skill to satisfy
the other person's deepest longings for fulfillment.**

Before we can understand the full scope of romance and seduction and the role it plays in a relationship, we have to define the components that create the emotion of love.

Love has always been a topic that's been elusive for most people to grasp. One of the oldest concepts regarding what love is came from Plato, who believed love was a yearning to develop togetherness. As people became civilized they created a sense of personal isolation and man had a deep feeling to fulfill togetherness. Love provides man with the togetherness of bringing two people into one union. This desire need for togetherness has long been the major belief of what love is. However, in the past 20 years, research has discovered the key aspects of the personalities that are directly involved with starting the flow of romantic feelings, or what we call love. Psychologists discovered that just three basic components of a person's basic identity are important. **They are gender, social persona, and self ideal.**

These components are the deepest aspects of everyone's identity. For this reason, these three variables have the greatest impact on a person's feelings and why they fall in love. Love is something that develops from within the person's own psyche. In other words, the stimulation of these three areas is what gives birth to love. **Knowing how to stimulate these areas is what we describe as seduction.**

Love usually begins on the basis of the chemistry between two people and how they are going to respond to each other's personalities. During the courtship periods, people will discover each other's characteristics and respond to the areas that are comfortable with their self-identity. As people become more involved and more passionate, they experience within themselves fulfillment of their needs and the personalities or social self-image will emerge. This will allow the relationship to gain strength and a sense of identity and eventually the people will feel complete and will fall in love with each other because in each other they see a reflection of both their inner desires and needs. The three key factors are:

1. Gender identify (masculine or feminine)
2. Social self image
3. Self ideal (characteristics of what a person truly is)

These three factors play a major role in whether a person will fall in love and with whom they will fall in love. Unfortunately, most people are not aware of this and have no idea what to look for in another person. They are attracted by superficial appearances and use a hit and miss technique of trying to make the most important decision in their life-find the right person for a long-term relationship. As society is proving today, lady luck does not usually stand by their side. Unfortunately, many of us go through this emotional journey of life from one relationship to another, continually searching, occasionally staying in a relationship until they discover that it is not the right relationship and then trying to recuperate from the emotional scars of that relationship before they can move on.

Self-ideal is the feelings one has of worthiness. Most individuals have a desire to improve and achieve. That is why part of the process of romance and falling in love is when the chemistry is right between people the self-ideal part of you will look for someone who supports, compliments and improves your self image and wholeness of yourself. Because love is very deep and involves very deep emotions, and because all of us want to have a satisfying and rewarding relationship, we must pay attention to the affairs of the heart and those things that pull against our heartstrings. Once you have an understanding of the components that make up love and once you have started into a relationship, you will be able to familiarize yourself with the aspects of personality in others and what is important for you to do in order to develop that relationship. You will be able to put together the information that we are going to outline to work to create the passion and feelings that you desire to create in your relationship.

Focus on the Other Person's Needs

You must focus on the needs of your partner because your goal is to get your partner to fall in love with you. Through romance and seduction your purpose is to find the best ways to satisfy the desires and needs of the other. When a person is in love they experience a sense of completeness—a pleasant satisfaction. This feeling is what develops in response to the person that they are with. In other worlds, when you reinforce your partner's self image, you create a state of well-being. The lover creates a feeling of self-esteem and satisfaction. The person's feeling of love many times encompasses their self worth, and you, in romancing and seduction, create that feeling of self worth and satisfaction. You validate the other person's value. Do not take lightly a person's need for approval. As our society has become more complex, everyone looks for approval from others. That is why belonging to organizations, groups, or social clubs gives a person a sense of worth. However, the greatest sense of worth comes from their lover. When somebody really feels loved, it causes the greatest impact on their self identify.

If you want to create joy in your partner, learn to respect their needs and their self identify and ego. Howe you feel about them has a very important effect on how they love you because it reflects directly on how they feel about themselves. Remember in the first section when we talked about the building steps in a relationship-do not criticize, give someone enough space and to have empathy for another person's feelings and beliefs? These building steps are necessary in order to develop a deep, strong relationship. When a person falls in love, that person's sense of self-identity and who they are and what they can do creates the depth and width of their love for you.

Even though people may feel they love someone because of the features or attributes that they have, it is really the feelings within their own mind that you have inspired in them, the qualities they desire and your admiration for those qualities in them has created the link between the two of you. Unless your lover feels valuable to you and to themselves, your love will not pass the test of time.

I have attempted to define, in a concise manner, the components that cause love, or the feelings of love in a person. The emotion of love is really a reflection of ourselves in others, and the links of our personality interwoven with another.

In order to develop a relationship with someone you desire, you need to apply the information that we discussed and how it will impact the other person.

Unfortunately, there are endless theories and books written about love. The purpose of this chapter is not to explore the entire world of love, but to give you a concise grasp of the key elements that compose the feeling of love with another person so that we can now explore the ways to use romance and seduction to fuel these components of love.

Cardinal Rule

Love and seduction deal with a person's self-identify and the 3 key components of love.
1.   Gender identify (masculine or feminine)
2.   2. Social persona (social self-image and role)
3.   Ideal self (self-ideal-traditional-unconventional or dysfunctional

Seduction

In essence, seduction of a person is being able to see and understand that person in the same way they see and feel about themselves in terms of their own self-image. Once you have accomplished that, you reinforce that self-image in the other person. That is what creates the elements of love.

Love grows out of the combination of components that are the basic part of each individual's self-identity. The three key elements, or components are first, the sense of gender. The individual as they perceive themselves, their masculinity or femininity and how they play those roles. Secondly, as Plato says, the sense of togetherness. Belonging with others. That is the social self.

And third, their feeling of their own self worth and potential ability. This is called the ideal self- image, or ideal self. These are the deepest and strongest emotional factors of a person. When you play these components as a harp string, they create the emotion of love.

A lot of people associate sex drive with love. As Freud describes it, the sex drive doesn't evaporate into thin air when it cannot be directly expressed. Instead, it will build into a sort of ground swell that comes out in the form of either sexual desires or romantic thoughts and feelings. However, what we are really describing is a person's gender identity and our need for sex without reason. It has put us in a position where we do not feel whole without an individual of the opposite sex. The acquisition of this other person or half creates and gives us the feeling of great pleasure that we call love. This view-point is supported by the reverse feeling of separateness, because being separated causes anxiety. This anxiety we call loneliness. When we overcome our loneliness and find the other half, we go from loneliness to togetherness to love.

We could discuss many ingredients or components that go into the recipe for love. However, the key ingredients are the ones we need to focus on. Although there are other ingredients that make up our self-image, the key components of gender, social persona and self-ideal are the predominant components that affect our feeling of love. These items affect us on such a basic level that the other components simply don't play as major of a role. This is the underlying reason why men and women do things in a relationship that can never be explained, or why two people in different circles are attracted to each other, and why throughout history people have done things in the name of love that could not be understood.

A seducer gives his loved one a feeling of self-satisfaction and self worth. That is the reason love directly touches the most important personal aspects of our self-identity. Love is not something that someone wears on their shirt sleeve. It is a distinct, internal emotion. It is a whole body experience. It is the experience a person feels when they combine the feelings of self- satisfaction, encompassing the sexual, social and ideal aspects of their identity.

Once you comprehend these components and how they combine to give the feeling of love, you are able to direct your actions toward the one you wish to seduce in order to accomplish the desired results.

The illustration below will show how romance and seduction play in the ring of love.

♡ Love's Path ♡

-needs-wishes =	empathy to find the =	satisfy your =	the emotion of
-desires-goals	really crucial needs	lover's needs,	*LOVE*
-longings	of your lover	hopes, longings	and joys

When a person is falling in love they are experiencing an all encompassing feeling involving the three key components of the personality and those components are being fulfilled and satisfied. Therefore, when you are romancing or seducing a person you are working on their inward feelings in which the sexual, social and personal identity of what they believe their ideal is have been stimulated, excited and then gratified.

Seduction is when you use your familiarity of love's components to create the desired responses. You become the seducer. The seduced has a belief that their personal value and desires are about to be appreciated and fulfilled.

The illustration below shows in a progressive manner what happens during the process of seduction.

Discover Their Longings =	The seducer understands, =	Seduced reaches a
Will he stay with me forever	appreciates and then…	level of satisfaction
Does he enjoy being alone with me	confirms the women's	and joy… result is a
Does he appreciate me	sense, or identify and	union of a man and
Does he think I look good	longings, thus creating	woman
Does he understand me	fulfillment and a sense	
Does he support my goals	of worth and self-ideal	
Does he feel we belong together		
Does he have the same values		
Does he feel I have worth		

I will try to explain in another way. Most people are thoroughly conditioned to act in a way that is in line with society's definition of gender roles. Each environment and culture create distinctive roles for each sex. As history has proven, people have the tendency to act out the roles society assigns to them. The Hite report strongly affirms that many of the characteristics of our gender roles are defined by our environment and culture. Once you realize this, you are prepared to understand that people are overly concerned about their bodies and their sexual identities. Very few people ever feel really secure. No matter what their experiences have been, people often feel unsure and compare themselves against standards of their gender or society. Therefore, men are always trying to secure and prove their masculinity and women are trying to prove and secure their appeal and femininity. Just look at any magazine and the ads within will substantiate this concept. As a result, everyone's sexual identity needs to be confirmed by a member of the opposite sex because we are disposed to a strong emotional reaction whenever we receive an approving response.

Whenever two people come together and are playing their sexual role and the other person appears a bit turned on, it supports, satisfies and gratifies the other person's gender identity. It is this support and gratification that we are each yearning for.

However, because of the different cultures, societies and environments that we have each experienced, how individuals obtain this gratification and affirmation is different. Everyone does not respond the same way to the same stimuli. For example, it is really our heart and our head that play a much greater role in stimulation than our lips and genital area. It is the process of that anticipation that many times will create great excitement or a romantic atmosphere. It is how we create this romantic atmosphere and seduce the other person that is important. There is a wide range of things that can be done to create a romantic atmosphere, but they will not always be received or appreciated by the other person in the same way, or create the acceptance and gratification. For some, the anticipation of a candle-light romantic dinner in an exotic place may cause feelings of desire. For others, the romantic trigger can be a picnic in a park, sharing a blanket at a concert, or relaxing on the deck of a yacht. The need and gratification for each is the same, it's just the vehicle or messenger that is different. That is where you, as a seducer, have to find out which vehicle to use to create the desired result. By working through the steps in developing a relationship that we have discussed, you should be able to have a feeling and direction of your lover's needs and wants. You should be able to anticipate what words, gestures or events will stimulate and gratify your lover the most.

Before we go on to discuss some of the techniques that you can use in seducing someone, I would like to point out that there is no firm rule or guarantee of certain results. In talking to many people over the years regarding different techniques that we have researched or experimented with, we find the responses are not always the same for a variety of reasons. People react differently to different stimuli because there is a great deal of anxiety and uncertainty involved concerning love. Unfortunately in today's society, a lot of men and women have not had good role models to learn from. Often, their environments are poor. Because of the high divorce rate and proliferation of broken or dysfunctional homes, many have been raised with a distorted viewpoint of what relationships, self identity and gender identity are all about. In many circumstances it can cause the person to become unreceptive to the normal stimuli, or may produce great anxiety and insecurity.

In today's society it is sometimes very difficult to understand and perceive the social impulses and individual needs because there is such a strong tendency in our society to be impersonal to each other. The close community ties that we had two and three generations ago have now been disbanded through our mobile society and through the onslaught of our media. Each day, through television and other forms of mass media, we are confronted with outrageous happenings and facts that it makes many of us not only feel apprehensive, but insecure. As a result it creates another layer, or filter, of apprehension that we have to work our way through when we are trying to seduce someone. That is why we are seeing more and more people actively dating and having a number of encounters. Such individuals often fail to find the person that is really their soul mate, the person who can create the kind of fulfillment and gratification that they are looking for. Anyone who is in their late 20's or 30's is probably already experienced this at least once in their lifetime and understands that a very strong physical attraction can be the beginning of a short lived relationship. Therefore, we must be careful and very conscientious to become good listeners and discipline ourselves to follow through with the steps in developing a relationship in order to develop the type of loving relationship that we desire.

Because lovers not only relate to each other on the surface with sexual acts, but through the emotional bond, the reality of today's world is that although the physical act of sex has become more permissible, fewer and fewer people know how to develop the true emotional love bond. Although we all have these feelings and impulses for romance, love and relationships, many of us only work on the surface level with the sexual ingredients of love and not with the deeper emotional ingredients. Without these deeper emotional ingredients, the love is shallow and will not pass the test of time.

Therefore, what the information regarding romance and seduction really tells us is that because of the tremendous deep feelings love creates, one of the most important goals that we can accomplish when we are seducing a person is to create a warm rapport. The object is to relate to one another in such a personal way that each feels that they belong with each other, and that each compliments and supplements each other's self ideal and gender requirements.

The real act of seduction occurs when one induces love in another person through encouragement and reaffirmation of their values and self ideal. This is the seducer's ultimate goal. When you accomplish this in the eyes of your lover, you have obtained a status above all others. You have created a bond and link that places you in a special realm. Although you may look and act ordinary to everyone else, in your lover's mind you are exceptional. That is why sometimes the simplest of actions or gestures can be so meaningful to your partner.

Ways to Romance and Seduce

Although love has many facets, the three key components that define and develop the emotion of love are within your grasp. You are in a position, through romantic gestures and ways of seduction, to influence the person that you desire to fall in love with you. What you have to do at this point is to concentrate on the underlying motives of your partner and show your appreciation and fulfillment of these motives so that your partner will feel both appreciated and gratified and respond in the affectionate way that we label love. You have to first be able to show your approval of the other person's physical attractiveness, giving them both a feeling of security and appreciation. Then you must respond to them in a particular way to create the rapport that says you both should be together and that you agree and support with their social ideal. Then you must be able to reaffirm those things that will validate and confirm the ideal side of their identity.

Basically, seduction is the capability of conveying to the other person both the appreciation of their self- ideal and the confirmation that you are pleased with the kind of person they are and the kind of companion they make. You demonstrate that you understand their characteristics and affirm that you appreciate the qualities and gifts they possess. In doing this, that person will be drawn to you because of the gratification that they feel and the satisfaction that you create in them. Thus, the bonds of love are created because of the pleasurable feelings that you have produced. To determine what techniques of romance will work for your particular seduction, you must take the time to listen carefully and find out the specific aspects of your partner's personality that you must appreciate and reaffirm. In order to do this you must go back to the steps that we discussed in developing a relationship. At this point, many of the steps that we have outlined that are important in developing a relationship will give you the key ingredients of where you can be most effective in seducing your partner in love. The steps in building a relationship will help you avoid the pitfall many people stumble into when they become mainly concerned about exterior qualities and their own self interests and desires. Remember, seducing a person is not about making your desires and likes the desires and likes of the other person, but of finding out what social impulses they have and showing how you can appreciate and fully gratify them. This is when you really show your skill as a seducer and a great lover. You have then gone beyond the surface and have become totally involved with their internal emotions and needs.

The seducer becomes more impressed with the inner qualities of a person then those that are on the surface. It is through the appreciation and gratification of these inner qualities that the seducer creates a bond of love. As a seducer you must learn the art of a subtle compliment, understand what excites a person emotionally and be able to appreciate that fact so that you are able to have sensitivity and react in such a manner that you accommodate the person that you want to fall in love with. You must be able to strike the proper chords of their desires in such a manner that will give them both satisfaction and excitement. It may sound like a lot at first, but once you are into the rhythm of romance it will become easier and easier. The joys that you will experience are worth the effort.

Applying Seduction

The reactions that you create while you are seducing a person is a result of the spontaneous process of the person's experiences from prior affairs and the degree of pleasantness or unpleasantness which they are experiencing as a result of support and confirmation that you give to their three fundamental pats (sense of gender, social self sense of belonging with other and self image—one's potential ability) that make up their self identify.

No emotion or reaction can be isolated from any given situation because a variety of experiences and identity factors come into spontaneous play. However, seduction can be used because we already are predisposed to certain romantic responsiveness. For example, because of our gender identity and ideal self image, when a woman tells a man he looks very masculine and handsome, the man would be predisposed to react favorably because it involves his need to confirm his sense of worth and masculinity has been appreciated.

Cardinal Rule

> **Affirmation of your lover's self-worth is the key tactic for evoking the emotion of love. However, do not over do it, or your words and actions will appear to be transparent or false.**

Our society by example from training from our schools, family and media make all of us react in a predisposed way to certain statements or actions. Boys are taught to act macho and aggressive in the pursuit of sex. Girls are taught to act feminine and be the caregivers at home. All these values are reinforced by our peers and media culture because all too often people are ridiculed when they do something different or wrong. For example, it would not masculine if a teenage boy cried because a girl did not call him when she said she would.

Understanding that people are in need of confirmation of their values and are predisposed to react in certain ways, we can now apply the different techniques of seduction to obtain the desired results.

Cardinal Rule

> **Seducer confirms Lover's self-ideal by appreciating their values.**

Everyone to some degree possesses this automatic emotional responsiveness. This process makes seduction possible. It is the conditioning of emotional responsiveness and a person's tremendous need to confirm their sense of self worth that enables you to seduce someone. When you appreciate one's values and worth and confirm those values and self worth and combine that with the three major components of love, you produce a feeling of not only self worth but satisfaction and joy in that person. This produces the emotion of love.

When you analyze the process we have just described, it begins to make sense why people will overlook many faults at times in both the individual and in the relationship because this underlying need for confirmation of their sense of self and identity is so commanding an emotion.

Although the romantic aspects of courtship are important in trying to create a nice environment, it is really how you affect that person that is important. Although superficial qualities such as appearance or wealth may first attract a person, it is not the building block on which you can build a relationship. **A word of caution**—do not ever fall into the trap that by believing you can make someone else fall in love with you, that you will fall in love with them. Real love is never certain. When you are getting involved with someone you may find that their priorities and self worth conflict with yours and it is impossible for them to reciprocate your emotions. Therefore, realize this early so that you do not create a situation of a bittersweet romance. Although the information we are giving you in this section will show you how to win someone's heart, you want to make sure that you are not setting you and the other person up for an emotional battle that will leave you both scarred.

Using the information that we've discussed will enable you to help distinguish whether or not a potential lover has the capability of returning the love and confirmation of your self worth that you will need in order to have a relationship bond and grow.

Working through the process to developing a relationship will assist you in recognizing the components and the inner character of the person you are courting. This is necessary so that you will be in a position to confirm their sense of worth. Sometimes people simply don't know themselves as well as they believe and it is only through communication and interaction with the person in their life that they will be able to recognize when they are really expressing a significant personal aspect about themselves. In some cases, because of the personality and character traits, some people may consciously protect their ego or be in a defensive mode because of having some emotional scars. In such cases, you will have to deliberately be more attentive to determine the true aspects of their identity.

Given enough time each of us will talk to a concerned listener and project their traits and their image of the type of person they believe they are. Once they have revealed enough, you will then be in a position to intentionally start the process of seduction by properly responding and showing your appreciation of their values and confirming their self-identity, which in turn creates gratification, satisfaction, enjoyment and most importantly intimacy. A word of caution—if you are too superficial or too anxious, and do not discriminate between the superficial values and the true values of self worth, you will not obtain the desired results. The strategy of seduction will only succeed when you sincerely put forth the effort to affirm the unspoken but deepest desire of your lover. Using the discussed techniques to develop a relationship will give you the opportunity and the insight to resolve the greatest needs and desires of the partner and enable you to complete the act of seduction by affirmation of their values and self worth.

One final note, love is very much like medicine. It is not a pure science that can be defined in black and white. There is a great deal of gray area. What we have attempted to do in a brief and concise manner is to show you the most direct path in seducing a person where you can create a feeling of love.

Another variable is that you may become so infatuated with the person that you are trying to seduce that you are seduced by them and your objectivity will not be clear. You may end up unknowingly making a lot of sacrifices or have the willingness to sacrifice your values to please them. However, in doing this it is very possible your needs will not be appreciated. Eventually your self worth and self- identity will not be fulfilled and there will always be a wanting on your part.

The following section will give you a general idea of how to apply the knowledge that we have defined and discussed in this chapter.

You must nurture your lover's self-ideal, but do it at a natural pace. If you try to rush the response you could turn the person off and have them withdraw. The growth of your lover's passion and emotion will begin when they recognize that you can appreciate their special value and worth.

This process will not happen every time you are together or as planned, however, with a succession of encounters the romantic bond will automatically build and will result in attracting your partner's heart and intention.

Cardinal Rule

> **The whole process of seduction is based in part on what a person is experiencing and feeling in their lives at that time, so depending on a person's prior experiences and mood, a comfortable, safe, romantic, exciting or familiar atmosphere may influence the results.**

If you are not currently interested or involved with someone, then start out with the idea of finding someone possessing the ideal traits you'd desire in a mate. Too often people leave their romantic involvement to pure chance. Many times circumstances work against the relationship, throwing up numerous obstacles. You do not wish to become involved in a bitter-sweet relationship because you'll end up always hoping that things will change for the better, and they never do. Too many people are attracted by outward appearances only and become emotionally involved with a person before they really find out the traits and qualities that they need or desire in a mate. That is why so many relationships are often doomed to frustration and anxiety. Do not allow yourself to fall into this pitfall. Do not be tempted by outward appearances only. Give yourself and your mate time to get to know each other.

Cardinal Rule

> **The seducer should find someone who possesses the qualities that they desire and admire in a mate. Then the seducer can truly appreciate and affirm the other person's self worth and value. Your desire will further enable you to seduce the person by confirming their self-ideal.**

When you relate to someone that you already admire, this will increase your ability to seduce that person because the motivation is greater. Using a realistic approach to seduce someone that you already admire and appreciate makes your job easier. The obvious reason is that you are more likely to create the love and relationship that you desire and that will stand the test of time. Although realistically you should have your preferences in order, it is important to understand that you will never find a mate that is completely perfect and meets all of your standards and expectations. Even the closest match will possess some characteristics that might irritate you. No matter how well suited you feel, you will have to compromise and adapt and work it out. That is why it is necessary to be careful in developing a relationship and to make sure that you work out any problems or opinions before you make a long term commitment. Realize before you are too deeply in love and try to overlook the faults and characteristics of the other person that these differences may turn out to be major obstacles in the future.

If you are patient and realistic and follow the techniques that we have defined in this chapter on romance and seduction, you can be fairly confident about your seductive powers. Once you've found the person you desire and have attracted that person to you, you will be able to develop the emotion and passion that you are looking for in a relationship.

Cardinal Rule

> **A lover gives the one who feels loved a valid reason to feel self-satisfied and fulfilled.**

CHAPTER V

▼

ON THE ROAD TO LOVE

You are now ready to go out and look for the potential love of your life. However, when starting out, make sure you take along self-confidence and the right attitude. Self-confidence and attitude can make the difference between success or frustration when you prospect for a new partner. Case studies illustrate that those who are overly apprehensive and have a lot of emotional scars or misgivings are more apt to communicate these apprehensions when they meet someone and are never given the opportunity to start a relationship. Also, people who have a negative, pessimistic attitude many times are predestined to fulfill their wishes and expectations of failure.

The first characteristic that other people are likely to pick up on is your attitude. By nature, people enjoy being around someone who is friendly, positive, relaxed and has reasonable expectations. This person is more suitable and you are then more likely to find and seduce that potential partner and lover.

However, as we discussed in the prior chapter there is always an element of chance and pure luck regarding the chemistry between two people. Do not be discouraged or upset if when you set out to find your partner the first person that you choose does not work out. Sometimes the initial chemistry just isn't right at the time for the two of you to become involved.

I usually tell this little story at my seminars to impress upon people that having the right attitude is essential when you want to get involved in a new relationship and an enduring relationship. Life is an emotional journey and when we start off our bags are filled with strong light emotions. We have trust, faith, love, hope, determination, pride and desire. And these emotions can at times make us fly along the journey of life. However, as time goes on we hit obstacles and end up picking up new baggage to carry along. That baggage is very heavy and is filled with despair, loneliness, pain, frustration, anxiety, mistrust, and greed. Sometimes we come to a major turning point in our life and we have to go across a very high bridge. For some of us who have all that old baggage with us, it is very difficult to cross that bridge because we must drag that baggage along with us. Others are able to walk across the bridge while some are able to run because they are able to leave the old heavy baggage behind. You must be able to leave the old baggage behind, no matter how terrible you feel your experiences were in a previous relationship. If you insist on dragging that old baggage into a new relationship you will weigh down the whole affair. It will not have a fair opportunity to mature and develop into the relationship you really want and desire. You cannot bring mistrust, anger and hatred into a new relationship and expect it to develop into a warm, loving, satisfying and fulfilling relationship. No matter how difficult it may be, you must conscientiously make the effort to free your mind from its apprehensions. Discard the old heavy, negative baggage and just retain the good, positive baggage that we start off with.

Cardinal Rule

A strong, loving relationship can make everything a little more bearable.

Realistically, you shouldn't make snap judgments about people and their characteristics or their outward appearance when you first meet them. That is why going through the 24 steps in the book, Love, Sex and Relationships, are so important. It gives you both the time and space to make a solid contact with a person and get their true reactions to your characteristics and needs. This is so very important if you want to avoid the situation that is commonly heard in divorce counseling. "He/she was an entirely different person after we got married. I never really knew him/her."

Personal rejection is a difficult thing for everyone. However, many times because a person doesn't accept your first invitation, it should not be taken as a personal rejection. Some people who are very shy will need a little time and space. Give them an opportunity to know the real you. You will see in many situations they will warm up and become comfortable. As we discussed in the prior chapter, a good seducer is also a good listener. You must be able to perceive the person's needs and longings so that you can appreciate and confirm them. Remember, someone may be a little shy, nervous or just having a bad hair day. Give them a second, or even a third opportunity. In between, try to let them know or see a little more of you. Find out the type of things they like to do so that your next encounter can be on familiar ground.

One final note, perhaps the other person is not ready to have love and a relationship enter into their life. Perhaps the other person has too much heavy baggage and cannot let it go. Do not become desperate and try to overcome all the obstacles in their life. There's nothing to be done until that person is ready to remove the obstacles themselves or make a change in their life. Experience has taught us that in the vast majority of cases you cannot change a person or remove their obstacles for them. You are better off keeping your self-confidence. There are many single people out there who are looking for happiness and love as much as you are. And you will be more prone for success if you look for a person who is at the same readiness level that you are for love and relationship to enter their life.

Cardinal Rule

Attempt to meet and socialize with people in places that you like and that make you feel good and comfortable. Chances are the person you meet there will feel the same as you. Visit places that have the atmosphere and the type of people and that put you in a good mood.

By conscientiously choosing the right atmosphere, your mood will remain positive and you can focus your attentions on the people you are meeting because you will feel comfortable and secure.

Cardinal Rule

When people experience the same reaction to something together they have a tendency to feel a closeness because in reality they are sharing a common emotion. Many times this will give each of them a sense of belonging and draw them closer together. When the seducer can create this emotion there will be instant gratification and the seduced will want this type of closeness to continue.

Another advantage of frequenting places where you enjoy the atmosphere and the people is that you are more likely to continue feeling enthusiastic and optimistic about meeting the right person because chance does come into play. You have to be patient. It may not be the first, second, third, or fourth day when you meet the right person. However, having the right attitude and being in the right atmosphere will keep your poise and mood positive and you will be prepared when that right someone comes along. Furthermore, take comfort in the fact that the vast majority of men and women have to deal with the same situation and lifestyles that you do today and most of them have the same yearnings and attitudes as you do. They are hoping and waiting for real love to come into their life.

The final step is also the first step, and that is overcoming your nervousness and anxiety in regards to meeting someone and starting the
process of seduction. Whether you start with a smile, a glance of the eyes,
or an overt approach, you must take that first step. If someone catches
your eye and hasn't noticed your presence, maneuver yourself in a place to
at least give that first glance, smile or eye contact. If it is received with a
like smile or eye contact, then follow up. It often doesn't matter what the
first remark is, but if you can't think of anything to say, a friendly "hi," can
always start a conversation. Once the conversation is started the other person will usually offer their opinion on something, and that is your signal
to pick up on the topic and follow through. Once you make the initial
connection you can change the topic and the conversation will move
along. During that first contact, people must make a decision if they are
going to see you again or not, and usually they have very little to go on. So
during this first contact, you need to make them feel that you are on the
same emotional and intellectual wavelength. This is the most you can
hope for in that first meeting. They will also have to make a decision to
take it on face value. This has to do with what we refer to as sexual chemistry and appearance. This may not always be the best basis to make a
judgement, however, this is what people usually do. The best you can
hope for during the first meeting is being able to possibly compliment
someone's gender identity. This can usually create a bond and an interest
to see someone in the future because affirming their gender identity has
produced a favorable impression upon them and confirms that you appreciate them for themselves.

Cardinal Rule

One of the deepest romantic longings a person can have is to meet another person who feels the same way about things as they feel, and to be able to share a happening, event or attitude together. This serves to bring the people closer together as if they were one sharing the same experience.

During the first meeting you will have a tendency to move on to different issues, sometimes issues generating passion. A word of caution—do not move too quickly into these matters because the other person may be too unsettled or nervous to give serious thought or concentration to these matters, or it may make them feel uncomfortable. Try to keep the conversation casual and look for areas where you can reinforce each other's gender identity.

Most of the time the relationship on its own will develop and eventually you will get to the point where you're going to ask for that first date. The first date, at best, is kind of an audition for each other. It can cause a lot of pressure sometimes for people to put on appearances and formalities. However, try to make your first date in a setting that will induce relaxation and communication for both of you. Most people think that a romance should be fast, exciting and adventurous. Many people want to be swept off of their feet by a new partner. They may try to create a rapid pace. However, this can create two problems. First, it may be offensive and make the other person nervous. Secondly, as we have discussed in the fundamental components of a relationship, moving too fast can many times get people too physically involved too soon. This is one of the main reasons why new relationships fail to get off the ground. Incompatibilities and problems come up very quickly in the relationship before you have had an opportunity to build a strong basis and a good line of communication and trust, which is necessary in order to resolve or mediate differences or problems.

It is during this first date that you as a seducer should be prepared to start developing the process that we have discussed in this and the prior chapter regarding romance and seduction. You will begin to set both the stage and the tone for the relationship. Be prepared because it may move along very quickly. Emotion is not something that you are always able to control or channel. It is important for you to keep the other person's attention and interest so you can apply the techniques that you have studied regarding seduction and romance. It is not good enough to think about something, you must act upon it. You must be able to verbalize your feelings and your intentions. Do not doubt yourself. If you do, your prophesy of failure will come true.

If you apply the things you learned in the components of a relationship, the 24 steps, and apply the basic fundamentals that we have outlined in romance and seduction, you will be well on your way to creating the emotional responses and feelings that you so desire in a relationship. Once you start the emotion going you will also be the recipient of love. This is the beauty of love. It is a self-fulfilling passion that nurtures itself if given the opportunity and will create mutual feelings of appreciation, satisfaction and happiness.

Cardinal Rule

Since the process of love creates many emotional responses, many times the seducer can become the seduced in a relationship because things will evolve at a very rapid pace and the passion between the people involved can cause such a stimulus to their gender identities and self worth that roles can easily be changed.

Chemistry and timing are important factors in the development of love. Sometimes a woman and man who are attracted to each other seem to have many compatible interests and attitudes, however, they are unable to develop an intimate emotional relationship. The usual reason that they cannot develop a closer relationship is because either one or the other or both has a great deal of anxiety and is reluctant to be honest and intimate with the other person for fear of being disappointed, criticized or ridiculed. Thus, they are unable to move on to the next level of emotional commitment. You have to realize that in some situations you may not be able to do or say anything that will change this. However, working carefully through the 24 steps that are outlined in the other book may create the bridge that is necessary for the relationship to continue.

Cardinal Rule

The master key to unlocking the deepest emotions is based upon the seducer's ability to discover the seducer's unconscious anticipation of what a romance and their ideal mate should be, and then to accept and confirm those feelings in the seduced. This can usually produce a torrent of emotion for the seducer.

CHAPTER VI

▼

DON'TS OF DATING: AVOID THESE PITFALLS

The following forms of thinking are negative and distorted and can cause a great deal of anxiety in developing a wholesome sexual relationship. Each of the following descriptions includes an explanation of how this topic can challenge or cause confusion in developing a wholesome sexual relationship.

Former Sexual Relationships

Although honesty is a key fundamental block in building a good sexual relationship, from interviews with support groups we have learned that in almost all cases, discussing former sexual relationships will create distrust, anxiety between the parties and frustration. It hinders a romance from developing. Some may think that boasting about former sexual relationships and activities increases their desirability. In fact, it can have the exact opposite effect. Some people will even emotionally hurt themselves because subconsciously this will lower their self-esteem. So unless there is something positive to be gained, a discussion of your prior sexual relationships should never be discussed when developing a new relationship.

Labeling and Over-Generalization

Using a label to describe your partner or over-generalizing about certain traits of theirs can cause adverse affects. We are not discussing words of endearment. We are talking about the derogatory labels that people will sometimes use in a relationship or the over-generalizations of certain activities that should be kept intimate. Sometimes we rush in what we're saying and we fail to understand our true emotions. Using labels when discussing activities or personality traits can cause a great deal of anxiety, self-pity or frustration. The end result is that it will act negatively upon developing a wholesome and rewarding sexual relationship.

Realize that some people can be very innocent and immature when it comes to the art of a sexual relationship. They should not be ridiculed or questioned, but encouraged so they feel comfortable and competent and emotionally able to handle the relationship. One should find ego-strengtheners so that you encourage and reaffirm the positive in a relationship. Doing this will pay big rewards in the long term.

The thing to keep in mind is that in the process of overcoming a social anxiety, people experience moderate amounts of frustration and fear and they will react to the comments and labels that someone puts on them. Saying, "you're dumb if you don't understand this," or "you're dumb if you don't like this," can seriously damage a person's view of themselves. Subconsciously they will think, "well I'm either bad at this or wrong," when in reality there is no truth to the statement. So avoid making your partner feel uncomfortable and allow them to develop their own feelings and expressions and enjoy the relationship without creating anxiety by using negative labels or over-generalizations of what they should feel or do, or how they should react.

Discussing the Ex

Discussing the ex-boyfriend, girlfriend, spouse, has very little merit and in most cases from research we have found that it will create anxiety and hang-ups in developing a long-term sexual relationship. And, in fact, from case studies, we learn that it may even cause the break up and disintegration of a good sexual relationship. The discussion about an ex causes a great deal of negative thought. Are people being compared and being put up to a standard? Is that person still emotionally and sexually involved with the ex? Is that person so desirous of the ex that they cannot focus on a new relationship? Will that person be able to leave the prior relationship and ex in the past and develop a new life? Unless the discussion of an ex has a constructive positive purpose, refrain from talking about them. Usually discussing past events, exploits and appearances of the ex only causes doubts in your new partner's mind.

Secrets

Keeping secrets or having your partner keep a secret for you is a major cause for fear and anxiety problems to develop and is a major road block in developing a good sexual relationship. Maintaining good communications between the partners is essential in developing a good sexual relationship. Therefore, do not place a burden upon the development of your relationship by keeping a major secret from your partner that would adversely affect your relationship, or by making your relationship conditional upon keeping a secret. This is especially true when the secret is kept from the parents or the children of the partner. This puts such a tremendous burden on the relationship that many times the partner will never feel at ease and comfortable in a sexual relationship. Situations should be discussed amongst the partners so that they can overcome their anxiety related to the reason of the secret, and then they need to learn how to manage the problem or the secret. In some cases involving more complex factors, the secret may make a meaningful sexual relationship unattainable and impossible.

Cardinal Rule

> **Keeping a secret often causes a situation to get worse and puts pressure on your relationship.**

Friends and Family

If you are embarrassed about having your partner meet your friends or family, then unconsciously you are telling your partner that they are not good enough in your eyes. It also implies that you don't trust your own judgement and that you have made bad moves in your relationships before. If you have these feelings, discuss them, cope with them, resolve the issues. If you cannot bring yourself to feeling comfortable and fond of your partner, then you will not be able to develop a good and meaningful sexual relationship. Having mutual respect and admiration for each other is another cornerstone in a good relationship.

Never tell your partner that you are ashamed of them. If you are, and if you say this, it will almost certainly create a great deal of anxiety and regret in your partner and soon mistrust and anger will come into play and make it very difficult for anyone to overcome these feelings.

Being Superficial

Be careful in using words of endearment or of proclaiming love too soon in a relationship. First, it is possible that you can create anxiety in your partner by thinking things are beyond the point that they are. Things may be moving too fast for your partner, and they may require more time to feel the same way as you do. Getting too emotional too quickly can cause you to stumble in developing a good sexual relationship. Also, using words of endearment or saying, "I love you," too soon in a relationship can make the other person feel that you are casual or shallow, and not really in control of your true feelings and emotions. This in turn can make them feel that you're not prepared to enter into a meaningful sexual relationship. Don't rush yourself. When the time feels right and you know for certain your feeling then be open and free. Then use "I love you," in a meaningful and proper way.

Careers

Do not make the mistake of mixing your sexual relationships with your career. Do not showcase your partner as an object of conquest. This can many times cause severe anxiety problems. The partner is put in a position of having the tough responsibility of constantly being "on stage" and this causes a great deal of anxiety and resentment at times. It also can create a feeling of being under-appreciated and used. A partner may spend years trying to be acceptable and pleasing to somebody else's standards or ideals. This is not what a good sexual relationship is about. No one should discuss sexual matters until it has been agreed upon by both partners to discuss a sexual relationship in a business or social atmosphere. This can also make a person tense and unhappy and uncomfortable and will eventually lead to resentment and anxiety because they will feel that they're on trial, that they are being tested and compared, and they have to give a special performance. All of this can trigger increased anxiety and frustration and create problems in a sexual relationship.

Lies

A good relationship can never be based upon lies. We are not talking about an innocent fib like, "yes you look good in that dress," or, "you look handsome in that suit." We are talking about the lies that cause self deceptions, usually in the form of unexamined attitudes, feelings or beliefs meant to protect us from our anxieties about sex and intimacy. But instead of keeping us safe they perpetuate fear and discomfort, preventing us from experiencing real pleasure and satisfaction. The lies take two forms. Lies we tell ourselves, like, "we must be having good sex, my partner is happy and satisfied although I'm not feeling anything and I haven't experienced an orgasm," or the lies we tell each other, like, "sexual relationship and sexual pleasure don't matter to me. As long as you're happy, I'm okay." When this happens, what we are really doing is trying to overcome our feelings of anxiety and fear and avoiding addressing our true feelings. Women more than men have a tendency to conceal and hide their feelings and lie about the relationship. They will usually put up with more and forgive more. They will many times try to convince themselves that their own needs are minimal and that they get pleasure out of giving pleasure. However, all of this makes a weak foundation for a good sexual relationship. A woman may honestly feel, or make her self believe, that during sexual encounters an orgasm isn't critical. However, sex without satisfaction and excitement will only lead to a weak relationship. Most of the time, women talk themselves into the thought because they are under pressure from the anxiety of keeping up with the partner's concept of what a sexual involvement should be. Some partners have a great deal of anxiety over intercourse, and as a result lie to themselves that sexual pleasure doesn't matter and a sexual relationship doesn't matter, rather than directly addressing the feelings of why they have these fears and anxieties. The anxiety and fear over sex can be shared just as easily by men as women. Many times people are scared to become involved and feel inadequate and unsure of themselves. They feel that it is a concept that's beyond them. Most times they just have to stop telling themselves lies and learn to relax, take some risks, and be willing to experiment to find the right things that create pleasure for both partners.

Some of the other areas of lies that we tell each other or ourselves are that, "if I had a better body I would have better sex. If I use some form of stimulant or drug that my performance would be better." Sometimes, because people are fond of someone, they are not sure how to communicate and hold back their real desires because they don't want to hurt their partner's feelings. If you fall into these lies and lack the self confidence to communicate your feelings to your partner, then these lies will become self fulfilling, and you will not be able to make your sexual relationship better. You will not be gratified by the act of intimacy and sex. In order to make your relationship better, you must be able to be direct, honest and express your desires as well as your fears, and be able to take some risks and open up to your partner. Then you will be able to have true intimacy and pleasure in your relationship.

Remember, sex will only get better if you take steps to make it better.

Religion

Discussing religious viewpoints and opinions is a matter that has to be handled in a careful way. If you criticize one's religious beliefs or viewpoints, you will alienate that person and cause them to become apprehensive and fearful of a relationship. You must be able to be mature enough to avoid making allegations or assumptions and sensitive enough that you can understand and appreciate the other person's viewpoint and feelings. Never try to discuss religious viewpoints in the heat of passion, but in a relaxed and calm manner without trying to hurt or reject someone's feelings and beliefs. Ask questions and bring out the facts that have to be discussed regarding changing one's feelings or viewpoints. Different religions have different laws regarding intimacy and sex. The couple's sex relationship can only get better if they are able to understand, accept, respect and work within the framework of their beliefs. Otherwise, the relationship will develop problems and you will never be able to obtain true intimacy if one or the other partner has feelings of fear, sacrificing, self-deception or guilt.

It will surprise many that when you discuss the different feelings and beliefs you have in religion, that many of the beliefs are very compatible. Differences regarding issues can be resolved without anger and frustration, thus laying the groundwork for a peaceful sexual relationship.

Cardinal Rule

Be careful to avoid the major reasons relationships and marriages fail: poor or lack of communication—money—blame and guilt—too much criticism—sexual problems—interfering relatives,—careers.

CHAPTER VII

▼

MEETING THAT
SOMEONE SPECIAL

Love At First Sight

Humans seem to be programmed somewhat like animals mating in the wild to fall in love at first sight, and no one has been able to clearly explain why and how this happens to some people and not to others. However, the one key ingredient in falling in love at first sight seems to be timing. The timing is everything. Both people must be prepared and willing to enter into a sexual relationship and be attracted to each other instantly. That includes the style or look of the person, the body odor, the pheromones, the personality and the person's love characteristics that we have outlined earlier, all come into play and match or compliment each other.

Traits that we usually do not think about, such as, does the person instantly remind you of someone who is close to you or that you think highly of, like a parent image. The fellow laughs like your father or the girl has the same kind of smile and voice as your mother. From experience, we have found that when two people happen to meet that many times it's characteristics like this that have first attracted them and then allow their chemistry and blueprint for love to take over. The meeting can be magical or mysterious. It can even be exasperating. However, if all the chemistry is right and if the timing is right, things will happen and you will get a rush of instant emotion. So understand it, enjoy it and go with it.

For most of us who have not found love at first sight, our major problem is just meeting that someone special or getting that someone special to notice us.

Before we can put our dating skills to work we must meet that someone special, thus the art of seduction starts with a little flirting.

A smile, a wink, a toss of the hair, a touch, can be signals of courtship and flirting. The true open smile is probably the most common signal used in the courtship process, however, here are some tips on catching the eye of that someone special you want to notice you.

Complement the person, figure out what attracts you to the person or what feature they have that you like and complement them.

Flattery is one of the best ways to flirt with someone. You must do it in a natural way and be sincere.

Flattery can be most effective when there is an element of surprise, when someone does not expect the complement.

Remember when you flatter someone you affirm their gender identity and that inflates their ego, so that fact that you mentioned the complement is delightful to the person.

Do not over do the flattery or the person will know you are not sincere and feel hurt and turned off. Being able to flirt with someone and pay him or her a complement takes practice it may be harder to pull off than you think, but try and you will do okay.

Learn to do "the look" or the "double take" the look that people see when they know that you have noticed them and are looking at them. The look is friendly and interesting. The look that makes people want to say hello to you.

You are saying by your look that you caught my attention and I am interested in meeting you. You can start something from across a crowded room, especially when they gaze back at you to say I have noticed you too.

You want to attract someone, so make some movement that can be both sexual and rhythmic. For women and men you can wet your lips in a sensuous way. Women can play with their jewelry or put on some lip gloss, dangle a shoe, or toss their hair.

Men can smooth their hair, twirl your drink, adjust their shirt, or do a masculine muscle flex.

You can do almost anything in a sensuous way so that it is appealing to the other person.

If you are with a friend and you want someone to notice you, get their attention by looking at them when they notice you. Learn over and whisper something in your friends ear, perhaps smile which whispering and looking at the person. It will make the other person wonder, and is that person saying something about me to their friend.

Whispering invokes intrigue and makes people want to be included.

Once you meet the person you wanted to, you may at the right time use the technique of whispering because this has very potent sexual overtones if done in the proper manner. Leaning over and whispering in someone's ear something flattering about them can be a potent force.

Change the routing. Life usually gets dull and boring because we do the same old stuff. We form habits because it makes life simpler but also boring.

So be adventurous, change things. Do things differently and people will notice and want to become part of the new routine. Automatically, people will become excited when you are around because you are doing something different.

It can be a new look, new way to wear something, new place to go, new sound, new book, new game, or a new idea.

New adventures wait for you, whether it be just a moment, a day, or a lifetime. So be the spark plug in the group and they will all love you and you will get noticed.

Keep people guessing, change your routine do not always hang with the same person or group. Back off at times and people will notice and appreciate you even more. It is nice to be dependable, but you do not want to be taken for granted. Change is the spice of romance.

Be creative. Another way to flatter a person is to find a clever or cute nickname to call someone. This shows that they are special to you and that you appreciate them. The nickname should not be too common and never meant to be mean.

Certain nicknames can also be a stepping stone to intimacy and romance.

When you want to get connected with someone new using names or events can create an instant bond and credibility, and add to your social profile. The name or event makes people feel connected to you in some way. People use this technique in both social and business interchange.

Use an unusual object to get noticed. A conversation piece is an easy way to break the tension when meeting someone new. Usually people will ask you questions about the item and this will start the conversation. This is an easy way to flirt with someone and is more discrete, because you are discussing an object and not the person, or yourself.

Learn to back off, this gives the person your meeting a chance to assess you if you seem to put too much pressure on the person you can appear to be threatening and bold and this can cause anxiety and rejection.

So relax and let the person go at there own pace and be relaxed this will make you seem more desirable.

If you are nervous about meeting someone then really try one of the flirting techniques to get the conversation started. Help yourself by limiting the time you are going to be with that person the first few times. Knowing that you are having a brief meeting will help you relax.

Remember you must make things happen. Usually nothing will happen unless you try.

CHAPTER VIII

▼

CHASTITY AND ABSTINENCE

Do you know the difference between sex, love and a relationship? Having a sexual relationship is one of the most important voluntary choices a person can make. It will affect you emotionally and physically. If you chose not to be sexually active and want to protect yourself, then abstinence is the proper decision for you.

Sexual thoughts and feelings are normal, everyone has them. Sexual desires go along with physical and emotional development, so do not be embarrassed or nervous by them. Following abstinence does not mean that you do not believe in kissing, necking, petting, stroking or that you have to stay away completely from the opposite sex. It refers to abstaining from sexual intercourse, usually until marriage. Some people feel that avoiding temptation is necessary to avoid physical intimacy all together. In general, if you are practicing abstinence it is unwise to get into a passionate situation where you're going to be tempted to fulfill your urges. Still it is important to understand that these urges and desires are normal and good.

Abstinence has many rewards. Being a virgin is something to be proud of. Chastity is a good basis for self esteem. It allows you to be free of any worry or guilt. It means that you will be safe from all sexually transmitted diseases. It means that you have given yourself enough time to make sure you are ready for the responsibilities that go along with a sexual relationship. Abstinence allows a partner to be more open and honest.

Cardinal Rule

> **Safe sex is *not* 100% effective, only *chastity* is 100% protection for your most precious gift.**

The key to developing a good relationship is to be patient. Going too fast emotionally and physically can damage the sexual relationship. One must be emotionally as well as physically prepared for the relationship. One must feel comfortable and consent to the relationship. Remember, physical sex does not make a sexual relationship. You must be truly ready and prepared to make all the commitments that we have been discussing in this book

Sex can cause a lot of pain and sadness when people think sex is love. Having sex does not create love, but having sex without love at the wrong time, without the proper intentions or relationship can cause a variety of negative feelings and leave one vulnerable to STD's and unwanted pregnancies.

You must learn to take control of your body and life—learn so say "**no**" to premarital sex.

Keeping a relationship going is hard work and do not rely upon sex otherwise you will be disappointed.

Sex can fool you for a while and lead you into dating or marrying the wrong person. Sex can create a strong emotional bond and make you believe that you are in love and have a whole relationship. Your judgment can become clouded, leading you to a commitment that ultimately isn't right for you. When the sex and romance fade and you come to realize that there are no lasting commitments, values or plans, only terrible frustration is left along with regret and sadness.

Learning to say "no" to unplanned sex will make you a happier person. People believe that their dreams will come true when they have sex with that special person, but usually if you rush your relationship and blindly follow your passion, it is not your dreams that come true but your nightmares as you watch your relationship crumble and loneliness and sadness take over.

Do not follow the path of regret. It is not enough for people to feel passion in a heavy caressing and kissing session and to express words of endearment. It must be true feelings. People often say words of endearment during a hormonal moment, it is commonly called "pillow talk". If you try to push a relationship, you may end up destroying the relationship because you are moving too suddenly for your partner. You may end up having feelings of guilt or of being used. You may end up emotionally scarred because the words of endearment that were said during the moment of passion turned out to be false. Frustration, anxiety and hatred can set in very quickly in place of what you though was love.

Learn to be mature, allow love and relationships to grow naturally. Learning to say "no" at the proper time can show how highly you feel about yourself and others and what a high value you place on your commitment and sexuality. You can feel proud that you have no regrets and have avoided frustrations, sadness and STD's.

Both partners should take their time to really get to know the other partner's plans, likes, desires, needs, feelings and morals. When it feels natural and right, you will know it. When it is time to make a real conscientious commitment you will feel good about the decision.

Give love and happiness time to mature and develop into a whole relationship. Keep a good reputation, stay healthy, have no regrets, avoid sadness, frustration and unwanted pregnancies, guilt and disappointment by following chastity and saying "no".

The status of one's virginity is a delicate topic that must be discussed in a meaningful way in order not to cause problems in the development of a sexual relationship. To wait to discuss one's sexual preferences and plans until one is in the midst of a steamy, passionate caressing session could cause some undesirable effects. One partner may feel rebutted by the other if they themselves are not a virgin. There may be a belief by one partner that the other is using their virginity as an excuse to not become involved in a deeper relationship.

Saying that one is a virgin at the inappropriate time will add to the confusion of a blossoming relationship. Before a developing love affair becomes too intense, discuss your feelings openly. Tell the other person what your true attitudes are towards sex and be direct in communicating to your partner what is agreeable to you. In this manner you can gain respect and admiration from your partner and the two of you can then work on the same level towards a meaningful and rewarding relationship. There is a wonderful and delightful world of sexual sensations and pleasures that can be enjoyed without having sexual intercourse. Until you are ready to make that commitment, you should be comfortable in the relationship that you are developing because you know what goals you want to obtain.

Chapter IX

▼

Safe Sex Procedures

Sex is a good and natural process, a wonderful part of a relationship and is necessary for procreation. However, too much information has been made available for you to be irresponsible about sex. If you are not concerned about your safety regarding a sexual relationship, then you are not prepared to enter into one. A concerned, intelligent and caring person will insist on safe sex until you known beyond a doubt that each of your are free from any STDs and healthy.

Safer sex does not mean eliminating sex from your life. It does mean being smart and staying healthy. It means self-respect and respect for your partner—talking about sex, knowing how to protect yourself, and taking precautions every time. Safer sex means enjoying sex without giving or getting sexually transmitted diseases. It is what you do, not who you are, that creates a risk for sexually transmitted diseases—and you can protect yourself by the precautions you take.

Your decision to enter into a sexual relationship will affect not only yourself, but potentially your partner, your friends and your family as well.

The two key words to keep in mind when making a decision are "respect" and "responsibility." Respect yourself and your body, and take responsibility for your own actions.

There are thousands of wrong reasons for entering into a sexual relationship. However, as we have discussed and try to convey in this book, you must be both emotionally and physically prepared. Think things through clearly, so that you don't feel uncomfortable and that when you get into a sexual relationship, it will be a good experience that will make you feel happy and whole. You must consider the potential lifelong effects of having sex.

Physical intimacy can be a warm, caring, exciting experience. It also requires thought, planning, and responsibility. Choosing to be sexually active requires we take precautions to protect ourselves and our partners from sexually transmitted diseases(STDs). It is important to make sexual intimacy as enjoyable and safe as possible.

Many people believe that if a person wants answers to their questions on sex, they can go to their parents, family doctor or teacher. However, the reality is that most people feel uncomfortable discussing the subject. Children rarely seek answers from their parents, the school system rarely has good programs on sexual education, and many churches rely upon the family and the parents for sexual education. As a result of this veil of secrecy, it is clear form many of the surveys and studies that have been done in the past 10 years, including the Kinsey Institute and Roper National Sex Knowledge Test, demonstrate that the vast majority of people of both sexes and all ages are either unaware or improperly informed regarding sexual relationships and especially sexually transmitted diseases, their causes, symptom and cures. This section is to furnish the information that is so overwhelmingly needed in our society today but is not readily available to those seeking answers to the questions and assistance in developing the most important decision in their life. Choosing the right partner and forming a long term relationship, is the most important decision one will make in their lifetime because it will determine 90% of the happiness or misery that they will experience during that lifetime.

Cardinal Rule

Safe sex is important to a relationship because it creates confidence and trust between the partners by reaffirming each other's value of self.

Abstinence from sexual intercourse is the only foolproof way of having safe sex regarding unwanted pregnancies and sexually transmitted diseases. However, the medical field does make a difference between dangerous unprotected sex and the concept of safe sex. Having safe sex is the only way to protect yourself against sexually transmitted diseases, which are very contagious. You cannot tell if a person has a STD by looks: in fact, many people that are infected look and feel fine and appear healthy. The infected person may be unaware that they are infected, or ashamed or angry that they are infected and will not tell anyone. Never even take it for granted, you must be responsible, use your head, not your heart until you are certain that your new partner is not infected. Having sexual intercourse even one time with someone who is infected can expose a person to sexually transmitted disease and aids. These diseases can cause infertility, sterility, genital pain and irritation, nervous disorders, and even death. STDs can be spread through almost any body fluid, therefore, vaginal, oral and anal sex can cause the spread and infection of an STD.

Cardinal Rule

When you become involved with a new lover, you must always practice safe sex until both of you have had a complete medical exam and blood tests for STDs. As a show of good faith show your test results and make sure you see your partner' results. *Never* take someone's verbal statement of good health. If your lover refuses to show their test results, immediately stop the relationship.

Simple and Safe

STDs are spread by infectious microorganisms such as bacteria, viruses, and parasites moving from one person to another. Different microorganisms are spread in different ways. Most travel only in certain body fluids like blood, semen, and vaginal secretions. Some sexually related microorganisms can be transmitted in saliva, and a few are spread by direct skin-to-skin contact. Making sexual intimacy as enjoyable and safe as possible means knowing what kinds of intimate contact transmit various STDs. Protecting yourself means choosing only safer sex practices, suing latex barriers against STDs correctly and consistently, or not having sex. You do not have to have sex with a lot of people to get STDs. Your chance of acquiring STDs increases when you have unprotected sex, no matter how many partners you have. **Always take precautions whenever you have sex.**

Condoms, unfortunately, have not traditionally had a good position in our society. They were "those things" you used to guard against pregnancy. However, because of the increased public awareness of sexually transmitted diseases in general and AIDS in particular, they are now in style and the safest and most preferred way to have safe sex.

Condoms, when used in conjunction with a spermicide, or spermicide cream, are extremely effective in not only preventing unwanted pregnancies, but in protection from unwanted sexually transmitted diseases and Aids. There procure are widely available and in some cases freely given out. There is no reason for anyone to have unprotected sex.

A large number of medical studies have shown that latex condoms, especially if coupled with a spermicide, can dramatically reduce the chances of becoming infected with an STD. This is not to say that condoms are guaranteed to be 100% effective. They cannot completely eliminate the risk of contracting an STD or of preventing a pregnancy. Nevertheless they are the recommended and the preferred method. These products are widely available, and in some cases freely given out. There is no reason for anyone to have unprotected sex.

The proper technique to use spermicide with a latex condom.

The most important rule regarding condoms is to put the condom on before the penis comes in contact with the vagina. Most people don't realize that the penis will extrude small amounts of sperm and fluid before the full fledged ejaculation takes place. This is sufficient to cause both pregnancy and the contraction of a sexually transmitted disease. Place the correct side of the condom against the head of the penis and unroll it all the way down to the base of the penis (if the condom does not unroll easily, you have it backwards). Pinch the tip of the condom as you roll it on, so that there is some empty space at the end, preferably one half of an inch. Try not to leave a bubble of air at the tip as this may cause the condom to slip or burst.

The condom is very thin and is designed for protection and to give as much sensitivity as possible to both partners. The best way to penetrate the woman is to wait until she is well lubricated, or use a water-based lubricant. A non-lubricated vagina is more likely to tear the condom.

Sometimes penetration with a dry condom or dry penis can be irritable and painful for the woman. After intercourse, always remove the condom and avoid spillage of its contents. Check the condom for leaks and discard it. **Never reuse a condom under any circumstances.** Some people believe that they can wash a condom and reuse it. This is unsanitary and may help to promote the very diseases the condom was designed to protect against.

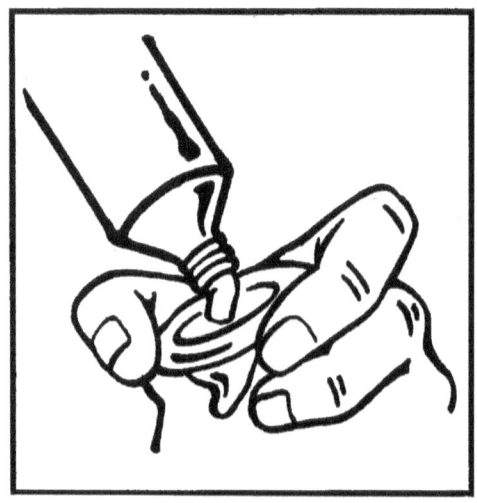

Proper technique to put on a latex condom

If you discover a leak, have your partner immediately apply spermicide to her vagina without delay. Do a proper washing. Medical studies have shown that even in the case of some sexually transmitted diseases, if the area is completely flushed out and washed with soap, it will destroy or remove the STD. If a condom breaks while being used to guard against pregnancy, then the woman should consult with her physician as soon as possible. You may be able to get a morning after pill, which can reduce the chances of getting pregnant if taken within 72 hours of intercourse.

Special notes regarding condoms:

Avoid using condoms that are more than two years old. It may have deteriorated and be more prone to breakage. Store condoms in a dry place away from heat and light. Unfortunately, many people are used to carrying condoms in a purse or wallet. These are bad places to keep them for any long period of time.

Never, under any circumstances, use petroleum based lubricants, like Vaseline, with a condom. Never use vaginal medications, including Monistat, Premarin, Estrace, Vagisil or any other feminine product. These products have a chemical in them that will cause the latex condom to deteriorate, allowing the passage of sperm and microscopic organisms. In the book Love, Sex & Relationships I discuss some exciting and exotic ways to put on condoms so that it can be a part of the foreplay and pleasure for both the man and the woman. Recently, researchers have developed a female product that serves as a condom. However, medical studies have shown that this device is not as trustworthy as a traditional, male worn condom. The female condom has a tendency to be pushed or moved out of place prematurely and, therefore, does not offer the protection that the traditional male condom offers.

How to Use a Condom Guide

Department of Health and Human Services, Food and Drug Administration

Follow these guidelines:

1. Use a new condom for every act of intercourse.

2. If the penis is uncircumcised, pull the foreskin back before putting the condom on.

3. Put the condom on after the penis is erect (hard) and before any contact is made between the penis and any part of the partner's body.

4. If using a spermicide, put some inside the condom tip.

5. If the condom does not have a reservoir tip, pinch the tip enough to leave a half-inch space for semen to collect.

6. While pinching the half-inch tip, place the condom against the penis and unroll it all the way to the base. Put more spermicide or lubricant on the outside.

7. If you feel a condom break while you are having sex, stop immediately and pull out. Do not continue until you have put on a new condom and used more spermicide.

8. After ejaculation and before the penis gets soft, grip the rim of the condom and carefully withdraw from your partner.

9. To remove the condom from the penis, pull it off gently, being careful semen doesn't spill out.

10. Wrap the used condom in a tissue and throw it in the trash where others won't handle it. Because condoms may cause problems in sewers, don't flush them down the toilet. Afterwards, wash your hands with soap and water.

Beware of drugs and alcohol! **They can affect your judgment**, so you may forget to use a condom. They may even affect your ability to use a condom properly.

One final note: Do not become confused by the word contraceptive. Many contraceptives are devices that are effective only in preventing pregnancies and offer absolutely **NO** protection against AIDS or other sexually transmitted diseases. For example, diaphragms, cervical caps and contraceptive sponges all prevent pregnancy, but do little to guard against disease. The only recommended protection for both unwanted pregnancies and sexually transmitted diseases is the traditional male worn condom.

Practicing safer sex means engaging in sexual intercourse that can potentially be dangerous. However, you can drastically reduce the risk by using the proper precautions until you and your partner have had an opportunity to have a complete medical examination and know for sure that you are healthy and STD free. This will allow you to have unprotected sex if you are not concerned about the pregnancy aspect. Safer sex allows you to enjoy sexual contact without acquiring sexually transmitted diseases.

You should always use a latex condom plus spermicide containing nonoxynol-9 when having sexual intercourse. When you start a new sexual relationship, chose your partner wisely, share sexual and medical histories and have the appropriate medical examinations done before ever having any sexual contact without a latex condom. STDs are transmitted through blood and certain other bodily fluids such as amniotic fluid, pericardial fluid, peritoneal fluid, pleural fluid, synovial fluid, cerebrospinal fluid, semen, vaginal secretions).

The following chart can be used as a guide:

RISK AND PREVENTION CHART

Amount of Activity	Amount of Risk	Precautions to Take
Abstinence	**NO RISK**	**No precautions necessary**
Sex with a single partner	**LOW RISK** If you have sex with only one person who also has had no other sex partner and neither of you has an STD, you have practically no risk of being infected.	**Use condoms during sex.** Wearing condoms are the most effective preventative measure sex partners can take. Men should wear condoms and women should insist male partners use them. Condoms are not fool proof, but they are usually effective.
Sex with a few people you know well	**SOME RISK** If you have sex with a few people you know well, your risk increases. You have some control over risk by choosing partners carefully.	Use condoms during sex. Use spermicidal. Wash after sex. Urinate after sex.
Your partner has sex with others.	**INCREASED RISK** If you have sex with only one person but your partner has sex with others, your risk increases. That is because you have no control over your partner's partners.	Use condoms during sex. Use spermicidal. Wash after sex. Urinate after sex.
Sex with many partners	**HIGH RISK** If you have sex with many people – particularly people you do not know well, you are at high risk of getting an STD.	Use condoms during sex. Use spermicidal. Wash after sex. Urinate after sex.

Cardinal Rule

Coitus interruptus—withdrawal of the penis from the vagina just before ejaculation is *NOT* an effective form of birth control and offers NO protection against STDs.

No matter how exciting a sex act is, it takes only one unprotected encounter to contract a sexually transmitted disease. No single sex act, no matter how pleasurable, is worth a lifetime of pain and discomfort.

Every situation and relationship is unique. Be honest and practice what you say, let your partner know your concerns. Emphasize that you care and want to protect both of you, sex is so much more fun when you have the peace of mind because you and your partner used proper protection and safe sex methods.

Safer sex can greatly reduce your chances of getting an STD, but sometimes infection may still occur. If you think you have been exposed to an STD, it is important to be examined, tested, and treated as soon as possible. Even if you have no symptoms now, an STD could cause serious health risks and problems for you and your partner later. People sometimes feel ashamed or guilty about STDs. Don't let your feelings stop you from getting help, or from letting your partner(s) get help. Medically effective, non-judgmental treatment and information (often free, or at low cost) is available from:

1. College/university health services

2. Public health departments or community STD clinics

3. Skilled private physicians

Condoms

Throughout the book we refer to condoms or latex condoms. Although there are a variety of styles and materials, the ONLY condom that we refer to is a latex condom. The preferred choice is a spermicidal latex condom.

Condoms are referred to as skins, rubbers and natural membranes. Although most condoms are effective to prevent pregnancy, the natural skin and non-latex condoms are perforated with microscopic holes or membranes that allow STD viruses to pass through. Therefore, the only condom to use for safe sex is a latex condom.

If condoms fail to protect it is mostly the fault of the user because they have used them in a slipshod, or improper way. Therefore, you must be consistent and follow the guidelines described in this chapter.

Lubricants and Application

Throughout the following sections of the book we will be referring to lubricants. Lubricants come in two categories. The first category are lubricants that contain a spermicide known as Nonoxynol-9. The spermicides in this category are used as contraceptives because they eliminate the effect of the male sperm on the female egg. Some medical tests have revealed that spermicides, especially ones containing Nonoxynol-9, are effective in reducing the chance of infection from certain sexually transmitted diseases. The second category of lubricants come in a variety of consistencies (water-based, oil-based, scented, colored, unscented, clear, liquids, gels, flavored) and are used primarily to enhance pleasure, **not** to prevent pregnancy or disease.

Never use oil-based lubricants with a latex condom. Oil-base lubricants will destroy the integrity of the latex condom.—A broken condom is useless as protection.

When purchasing a lubricant, read the label and see what ingredients are listed. Make sure whether it is either an oil-based or a water-based product. Be aware of any active ingredients in the lubricant that you may be allergic to, as this will cause an irritation or a rash. Be wary of some of the new products coming on the market that are silicone based lubricants. These products are made with Dimethicone and do not have any protective value whatsoever.

Lubricants used with latex condoms can prevent the discomfort associated with dryness during intercourse and also make condoms less likely to break. Water-based lubricants, like KY jelly ®, and various spermicidal jellies, are strongly recommended.

Sexual intimacy does not necessarily mean only sexual intercourse. You can engage in sexual activity that would still involve risk regarding STDs. For example, you can contract a sexually transmitted disease by having anal sex or oral sex. Therefore, all the information that we discussed regarding safe sex applies to all forms of sexual intimacy.

In order to have oral sex you should always use a latex condom and in the case of oral sex on a woman you should use a dental dam or latex barrier. If necessary you can cut a male condom into a latex barrier and use it as a barrier when performing oral sex on a woman. It is always advisable to use a latex condom with spermicide and lubricant when performing anal sex.

CHAPTER X

▼

MAKING SEX SAFER

If you decide to be sexually active you must be honest and communicate with your partners and insist on practicing safer sex.

The only completely effective method of preventing sexually transmitted diseases and pregnancy is abstinence. For those unwilling to engage in abstinence, it's essential to practice safe sex.

Communicating with your partner about your concerns, fears, desires, and choices are essential to making sex safer. Do not be afraid to ask about your partner's health and sexual history. Honesty on your part communicates that you are and promotes honesty from your partner; you both can them make informed decisions. But remember—**it's up to you to protect yourself in every sexual relationship**. Don't depend exclusively on talking to protect yourself from STDs. Your partner may not realize, or reveal, things that could put you at risk for STDs. Together decide what you both feel comfortable doing sexually, and what precautions you will take. It is okay if you feel awkward or uncomfortable talking about sex. Sharing those feelings with your partner helps. Talking about sex can be easier if you are bale to talk about other personal and emotional issues. Being intimate is much more than a sexual act. If discussions about relationships, emotions, or sex are difficult for you, seek counseling from capable professionals who can help you learn some important skills in communication.

Safer Sex

Kissing, hugging body rubs while partially dressed, back rubs, foot rubs, caressing, nibbling at each other's bodies except for the genitals or anus, talking bout sexual fantasies, dry humping, showering together, licking or fondling your partners body except for the genitals or anus, giving an oil or lotion massage, stroking your partner, manual stimulation to your partner's sex organs as long as you have no cuts, abrasions or open sores. Preferable if you are going to have an orgasm you should use a condom whenever possible, rubbing your bodies together as long as there is not broken skin on your partner's body. Using your hands to masturbate each other making sure that you do not ejaculate in or near any of your partner's body orifices, or touching each other while sleeping together.

If you are going to do anything more than what is outlined above, you need to honestly communicate with your partner about the safe sex precautions.

The following are some ways to bring up the topic of safer sex with your partner before you get too involved.

You plan the moment. Do not wait until the middle of a passionate moment when your passions are running too fast and your hormones have taken over.

First, when you are by yourself—practice what you want to say because talking about safe sex sometimes makes people very embarrassed and nervous. Give yourself some time and try rehearsing. Pretend you are playing a role with your partner. Then try to find a private, comfortable, cozy place where you feel at ease and can talk privately with your partner. Here are some suggestions on how to start the conversation.

You could start off by saying "A lot of people are talking about using condoms and how they protect. I think it's a good idea. How do you feel?"

If your partner is resistant and says something like, "I don't want to talk about it," or "forget it," or "I don't like condoms," you can say, "Why do you dislike condoms? Can't we give them a try? Do this for us."

Another approach would be if you're already involved, you could start off by saying "I don't want to give up sex but AIDS and pregnancy have me scared. I'm going to use condoms whenever I have sex." If your partner resists and says something like, "don't you trust me?" or "do you think I have a disease?" or "don't you think I know better?" you can respond by saying, "I do trust you but how can I be sure of your former partners or mine? Trust has nothing to do with pregnancy."

Another approach, "I have been thinking a lot lately about all the diseases that you can get when you have sex, but if we use condoms and spermicide we can prevent them." If your partner replies, "I don't like condoms, they're no fun," or "they destroy the spontaneity of sex." or "I think condoms are stupid" you can say, "Well, I will keep them with me and it could be fun if we put it on together. Let's give it a try because I want to do this or I need this." Try to put it on an equal level so that both people are agreeing and know that it is for the best for both people.

Another way is to propose "I'd love to make love with you, but I always use condoms to play it safe." If your partner is unsure or resists or says something like, "I think it's going to ruin the feeling for me," or "it's not macho to use condoms," you can reply, "it might feel a little different, but let's try it. After all, sex won't feel good at all if we never have it. We need to use condoms and a spermicide."

Plan ahead. If you feel you are going to have sexual contact make sure that you take along some spermicide and condoms. Don't depend on the other person. Play it safe. After the first several times you both will have a peace of mind and you'll find that having sex is more enjoyable when you feel safe and secure. Your partner may try to talk you out of it but remember that no sex, no matter how great you think it might be, is worth a lifetime of pain and suffering or even death. It is possible to become infected or pregnant if you have just one unprotected sex act.

CHAPTER XI

▼

SEXUAL HISTORY

Good communication between partners is essential to make sex as safe as possible and to dramatically reduce the risk of contracting an STD.

It is hard to talk to your lover about sex, past sexual habits and medical history because at best most people are embarrassed and they will probably sound like they are judging or criticizing. There is also enormous cultural and religious barriers that keep men and women, for different reasons, from talking about sex with each other. Even our society makes it difficult for men and women to talk to each other about sex. Men are suppose to know everything about sex, it is not macho to discuss sex with a woman. Women, on the other hand, were brought up to believe that you are not a lady if you talk about sex. Responsible, caring adults must talk about sex and medical history before hand. Chapter Two thoroughly explains the methods about honest communication between partners.

Safe sex is not possible until both partners have had a medical exam and blood test and have tested negative for ALL sexually transmitted diseases and waited the appropriate incubation period to ensure a clean bill of health. During the waiting period both people must not engage in any sexual activity or IV drug use.

The partners should agree up front to practice safe sex using condoms and spermicidal until he exams are completed and both are free of any STD. Practicing safe sex by having a medical exam and blood test only relates to STD's and does not protect women from unwanted pregnancy.

If you feel that you do not know the person well enough to discuss such things, or do not feel comfortable to discuss these things with your partner, then you have to ask yourself the question, should you really be developing a sexual relationship with someone you cannot talk to about sex and your emotions.

Precautions You Should Take Regarding Sex

Learn to communicate effectively with your sexual partner.

Never mix alcohol or drugs with sexual activity: use humor and honesty instead.

Choose lower-risk sexual activities

Use latex barriers to prevent exchange of semen and vaginal secretions. Be sure you know how to use condoms correctly and understand their advantages and limitations. Learn about lubricants.

Remember that contraceptives other than condoms (including birth control pills, intrauterine devices, and diaphragms) do **NOT** protect you against STDs. To prevent both pregnancy and STDs, use a condom along with the other contraceptive methods. **Precautions cannot eliminate all risks, but you can make sex much safer.**

CHAPTER XII

▼

SEXUALLY TRANSMITTED DISEASES SEXUALLY TRANSMITTED DISEASES—WHAT ARE THEY?

STDs (Sexually Transmitted Diseases) sometimes called Venereal Diseases are infections you get from sexual contact with a person carrying the infection. More than 25 STDs have been currently identified.

Sexually transmitted diseases (STDs) are infections you transmit or receive during unprotected sexual contact. There are many: chlamydia, gonorrhea, genital herpes, and infection with HIV (the virus that can cause AIDS) are just a few. Some STDs spread more easily than others. You never become immune to STDS. You can get re-infected and you can have more than one STD at the same time. Some STDs show few or no symptoms: many people are infected and spread the microorganisms without knowing it.

One STD, hepatitis B, is preventable by vaccination. There is effective medical treatment for many other STDs, like chlamydia and gonorrhea. There is only limited therapy for viral STDs, like genital warts (which are caused by human papillomaviruses), herpes, and HIV infection.

STDs are at an epidemic rate in the United States today. They are among the nation's most common and contagious diseases, affecting at least 40 million Americans. It is estimated that there are about 12 million new cases per year.

Who is at Risk for STDs?

Any sexually active person is vulnerable to contracting a sexually transmitted disease. If you have unprotected sex the risk is greatly increased. No one is immune. It is estimated that 1 in every 6 adults in the United States has had or does have an STD. Even though many of these STDs are curable, many are not. Even among the more treatable ones, repeated infections can often toughen the virus responsible to the point where it becomes resistant to treatments and medications.

Please do not use this information in this section to self-diagnose or treat yourself. **If you have any symptoms or suspect you have an STD, get medical care promptly and take the time to follow-up after your complete treatment to make sure you are cured.**

Are There Warning Signs or Symptoms of STDs?

Most STDs have symptoms or warning signs of some sort. It's important to pay attention to any and all signals that your body sends you. However, sometimes the symptoms are so mild that they go unnoticed, especially in the case of women. Therefore, if you have had sex with someone who might have a STD, the only sure way to determine infection is a blood test and exam from a doctor or other medical professional.

Because STDs can effect anyone it is important to know what to look for in yourself and others. Be especially alert to body changes in the genital areas. Sometimes these warning signs might appear right away or they may not show up for weeks or even months. Sometimes the symptoms will not appear or they will appear and disappear; however the disease is probably still active. STDs do not go away by themselves, therefore do not be lulled into a sense of false security if the symptoms disappear. You must have proper medical treatment.

Risk Factors

Sexually transmitted diseases such as aids, syphilis, hepatitis, gonorrhea, venereal warts, chlamydia and herpes are no longer someone else's problems. STDs are now everyone's problem, including teenagers. Many infected people are symptom free and may unknowingly pass infections on to others. Even if you think your partner is not that kind of person who would have an STD, you can't be sure because when you sleep with someone, in a way you're sleeping with all of their past partners as well.

Personal Exam For Risk

You are not at risk for STDs if you're **NOT** sexually active and practice **abstinence.** You are probably not at risk if you have been in a long term relationship for ten years or more and neither you nor you partner has had other partners, received a blood transfusion or blood products, used IV drugs or has come in contact with an infected person through their occupation.

ASK YOURSELF THE FOLLOWING QUESTIONS TO DETERMINE WHETHER OR NOT YOU ARE AT RISK

1. How sure can I or my partner be that neither one of us is infected with AIDS or another STD?

2. How sure can I or my partner be that our past partners were not infected?

3. Have I been sexually active with more than one partner in the past ten years?

4. Is it possible that my partner has been exposed to IV drugs or received a transfusion of blood products since the late 1970's?

5. Can I become infected with STD by sleeping with an infected person only once?

6. Do I practice safe sex?

7. Did I discuss STDs and medical history with my partner before having sex?

STDs are a fact of life. If you are sexually active you're at risk regardless of your age, race, occupation or sexual preference. Furthermore, that risk is increasing because more and more people are getting STDs and new STDs are also being identified. The key to reducing your risk is to be informed about STDs and how to prevent them.

This book is not intended as a substitute for professional medical care or a thoughtful consideration of the personal medical risk involved in sexual expression today. If you suspect you have an STD, get medical care promptly. Control and safety are the major items regarding STDs. First you must learn about STDs. Second, you must recognize their symptoms and the body's warning signals. Third, you must get early and proper medical treatment, and fourth you must learn how to prevent STDs by practicing proper prevention techniques.

STDs

The following is not an all-inclusive list of STDs; however, the main ones are outlined for your assistance in this booklet. They are as follows: herpes, condyloma (venereal or genital warts), chlamydia, AIDS (acquired immune deficiency syndrome), gonorrhea, hepatitis, syphilis and vaginitis.

Symptoms

Recognizing symptoms is the most important way of controlling the spread of STDs. Symptoms are your body's way of telling you something is wrong. Be especially alert to changes in your body. When something feels or looks different seek prompt medical care. If you are a woman you must be especially careful because sometimes early symptoms of an STD are noticeable in men but not in women. Frequently, a woman's first clue that she may have an STD is learning that a sex partner has one.

Most STDs can be cured if treated early. Women of childbearing age need to be particularly alert. STDs frequently cause problems with reproductive organs, making it difficult or impossible for a woman to get pregnant. In addition they're capable of causing diseases in newborns.

How Can I Get More Information?

You may obtain additional information about STDs by writing to the STDs Foundation, P.O. Box 511, Troy, Michigan 48099. Another phone resource is the VD National Hotline at 1-800-227-8922. In California call 1-800-982-5883 or the AIDS Hotline 1-800-342-AIDS.

Early Diagnosis

Early diagnosis gives a person the best chance for successfully treating an STDs. Even if a disease can't be cured, it can often be controlled. Here are some important things for a person to keep in mind if they've noticed any symptoms:

Eight Step Program

1. Be sure to be completely open with your doctor about what areas of your body have been bothering you.

2. If you have an STD then talking with your partner can be difficult. Ultimately though it is the most caring thing you can do and the only way to avoid becoming re-infected.

3. As soon as you are diagnosed, take a quiet private moment to discuss your treatment with your physician and then explain to your partner(s)

why they need an evaluation and possible treatment. Encourage you partner to seek treatment, too. Try not to pry into each other's past or place blame but be honest and show you care.

4. Make sure that you take the current medication prescribed by your physician and use the medication in the manner you are supposed to.

5. Go back to your doctor for a follow-up exam and tests according to his or her instructions.

6. Make sure you don't share your medications with someone else. Everyone should consult their own physician as to the proper medication and dosage.

7. Make sure you consult with your doctor to be reassured that you are cured or have the STD under control. Viruses are known for lying dormant and flaring up. The chance of this is increased if one hasn't gone through their whole prescribed treatment.

8. During your period of treatment you may be asked to abstain from sex or take other precautions. Consult with your doctor to find out when it is safe to have sex again. Don't have sex until you and your partner are completely cured.

Guide For STDs

This guide to STDs was prepared to help you better understand STDs, what they are, their symptoms, treatments and if they are life threatening. Knowing about and understanding STDs is the proper way to ensure a happy and healthy sexual future.

HERPES SIMPLEX VIRUS (HSV)

Herpes is actually a family of viruses that causes a variety of diseases that almost everyone comes into contact with. Examples of such ailments are chicken pox, mononucleosis and fever blisters. The herpes simplex virus or genital herpes usually affects the mouth or the genitals; it is the simplex virus that is an STD. Over 40 million people have herpes. This viral infection is so widespread that support groups for people with herpes have formed in many cities. At present the infection has no cure and, understandably, many worry about herpes. Many people get only one outbreak while others must learn to control the infection.

Symptoms—The first episode usually occurs from 2 to 21 days after exposure. Symptoms may include swelling, pain, itching or burning at the site of the infection. This is followed by reddening and finally tiny blisters, which may then burst forming tender ulcers which crust and eventually heal. Some of the additional symptoms that may be experienced are fever, chills, lethargy, muscle aches or headaches. Some may have a burning or tingling feeling during urination or have a discharge of a liquid-like substance. Herpes sores come and go, but the virus remains. Symptoms begin with one or more fluid-filled blisters that open into sores. Sores may be painful and accompanied by swollen glands. Oral herpes produces sores around the mouth, genital herpes produces sores around the genitals and buttocks. The sores or blisters first open then heal as new skin tissue forms. During a first outbreak the area is usually painful and may itch, burn or tingle. Herpes may also infect the urethra, and urinating might cause a burning sensation. The first outbreak might last up to several weeks. When the sores are completely healed, the active phase of the infection is over. Symptoms may vary form one person to the next and in some people the first infection is so mild it goes unnoticed. Even so, subsequent re-occurrences of the disease could cause sores to reappear. Be aware that some people who have herpes have very minimal symptoms and do not seek medical treatment. Some people have frequent re-occurrences, while others have them rarely. Re-occurrences generally decrease as time goes on.

Treatment—Herpes can't be cured, but it can be controlled. Drugs called Acyclovir or Zovirax may speed healing and prevent re-occurrences. You can help, too. Keep herpes sores clean and dry, and don't scratch them. Pregnant women who have herpes should tell their doctors so that precautions (such as Cesarean delivery) can be taken to spare the baby from being infected.

Prevention—To prevent getting or spreading herpes, avoid sex during flare-ups and learn to recognize the sores. If you touch a herpes sore, wash your hands before touching your eyes, your mouth, or your partner. Use a condom between flare-ups. Reduce the stress in your life, too. Stress can trigger herpes outbreaks.

Condyloma (Venereal Warts)

Genital warts occur most often in young, healthy, sexually active men and women—especially in couples who don't use protective condoms for birth control. Without treatment, these warts cause cellular changes that could progress to genital cancer, especially in the cervixes of women. If you're pregnant, warts can be transmitted to your infant or block a normal delivery, so that a Cesarean (surgical) delivery may be needed. If you and your partner aren't both treated, you're likely to pass the virus back and forth to each other (the "Ping-Pong" effect).

Symptoms—Venereal warts can be flat or shaped like little cauliflower. They grow on the penis, vagina, and cervix and in and around the rectum and throat. The growths may take months after exposure to appear, and often they're so tiny they go unnoticed. Since they're hard to see, especially in the vagina or rectum, a thorough medical exam may be necessary to diagnose them.

Treatment—Venereal warts are more difficult to remove when they're bigger, so don't delay. They're usually removed with chemicals such as podophyllin (except on pregnant women). Sometimes warts are frozen off with liquid nitrogen or are surgically removed. Repeat treatments often are necessary to remove all warts. A single wart can multiply into many.

Prevention—To prevent venereal warts, use condoms, know your partner and get regular medical exams. Also, learn to manage stress—outbreaks of venereal warts may be related to your stress level. Pregnant women should be especially cautious as babies can be infected with venereal warts during childbirth.

AIDS

AIDS is the deadliest STD. The virus destroys the body's immune system, making a person vulnerable to attack from thousands of other viruses. Many people who have the HIV virus don't have AIDS, but they can pass it on. High-risk groups include gay and bisexual men, people who share IV needles, and sex partners of these groups. AIDS is spread through exposure to infected blood or semen, not by casual contact.

Symptoms—Swollen lymph glands, fever, night sweats, severe fatigue and weight loss. Many AIDS symptoms are similar to those of other diseases except that AIDS symptoms persist and get worse. If you get sick often or if an illness lasts a long time, seek medical care right away. The AIDS virus attacks the body's immune system and leaves the person with AIDS unable to fight off many other kinds of infections and cancers.

Treatment—If you're experiencing AIDS symptoms, see a doctor immediately. Currently AIDS has no cure and no vaccine, but treatments are being tested. For information, call the AIDS 24-hour hotline at 1-800-342 AIDS or the Gay and Lesbian Crisis Line at 1-800-221-7044.

Prevention—If an infected partner's blood, semen or vaginal fluids enters your body through a break in the lining of the rectum, vagina, mouth or through a needle puncture, you can be infected with the virus. You may not know you have cuts or sores in these areas as they may not hurt or even be visible. Reduce your risk of getting AIDS by avoiding exposure to a partner's bodily fluids (blood or semen) by using a latex condom plus spermicide. Never share an IV needle under any circumstance. Do not allow body fluids to contact the skin.

Gonorrhea

Gonorrhea is so widespread, a new infection occurs every 12 seconds. If untreated, gonorrhea can cause sterility and, in women, pelvic inflammatory disease (PID.)

Symptoms—The incubation period for men is one day to two weeks and is generally longer for women (7 to 21 days). Men may notice a milky white pus discharge and painful or tingling urination. Women often have no early symptoms, but later they may develop a painful burning sensation during urination or a yellowish or whitish vaginal discharge. Left untreated, these symptoms may generate into abdominal pain, bleeding between periods, vomiting and fever. If left untreated, the real danger is that the infection will ascend into the seminal vesicles, the rpididymis or the prostate, potentially causing sterility. It can also cause a narrowing of the urethra, making urination permanently more difficult. In women the bacteria will invade the reproductive system, usually the ovaries and fallopian tubes, causing pelvic inflammatory disease. This can cause infertility. The bacteria in both men and women can sometimes get loose elsewhere inside the body and attack heart valves, the brain, joints or the blood stream. Pregnant women can pass the disease on to their babies during childbirth. Many states require infant's eyes to be treated with special silver nitrate or penicillin eye drops to prevent infections that can lead to blindness from gonorrhea.

Treatment—Gonorrhea is a bacterial infection and can be quickly cured with antibiotics. However, some gonorrhea germs are penicillin-resistant.

Prevention—The best protection against gonorrhea is to know your sex partner. If sexually active, learn the symptoms of the infection, use condoms and other precautions to reduce risk, and get regular medical checkups.

Vaginitis

Vaginitis is really a group of diseases. The three most common are trichomonisas, yeast infection, and gardnerella. Although mainly a woman's problem, vaginitis can be carried and spread by men. In fact, trichomoniasis is often called "Ping-Pong" because sex partners don't know they have it and keep re-infecting one another. Some forms of vaginitis, such as yeast infections, also occur in women who are not sexually active.

Symptoms—The vaginitis disease all shares a common symptom discharge. Trichomoniasis produces a frothy, yellow discharge and causes persistent itching or burning. The discharge may have a unpleasant odor. Yeast infections produce a discharge that looks like cottage cheese and can cause an intense itch. Gardnerella causes a grayish-white, watery, strong-smelling discharge.

Treatment—Both you and your partner should be treated for trichomoniasis to avoid re-infecting each other. Trichomoniasis is treated with a medication called metronidazole. Yeast infections are treated with nystatin vaginal suppositories or creams. Gardnerella is treated with ampicillin or metronidazole. Be sure to take all the medication prescribed for you.

Prevention—Vaginitis can be difficult for a woman to prevent. These precautions will help to reduce the risk. Wash the vaginal area daily with soap and water, rinse, and pat dry. Don't us douches or strong deodorant soaps. They can upset the vagina's natural chemical balance, permitting the growth of yeast. Wear cotton or cotton-crotch undergarments. They provide better air circulation than other types of materials, which discourages infections.

Syphilis

Syphilis is caused by corkscrew-shaped bacteria. Unless treated, it can cause heart and brain damage, even death. Pregnant women can give the infection to unborn babies.

Symptoms—The first symptom of syphilis is a painless sore, which may not be noticeable. Later symptoms include rash and fever. Those symptoms disappear but, if untreated, the disease leads to serious damage years later.

Treatment—Syphilis is treated with antibiotics. Early treatment is important because although symptoms of the infection may disappear, the disease remains in the body and progresses to the next stage of severity.

Prevention—As with gonorrhea and other STDs, knowing your sex partner is the best prevention against syphilis. If sexually active, use condoms and other precautions and get regular medical exams.

Chlamydia

Chlamydia is the fastest growing STD, especially among young people 15 to 25. It's already more widespread than gonorrhea. It may be overlooked because it's often symptomless and may not be tested for. In women it may not be noticed until its later and more serious stages. If untreated, chlamydia can cause sterility in both women and men.

Symptoms—Chlamydia can be like a time bomb. At first, it's symptomless, then complications flare up. When early symptoms do appear, they're often mild. These symptoms could take the form of an odorless discharge or burning. A complication in women is pelvic inflammatory disease (PID), a major cause of sterility and ectopic (tubal) pregnancy. PID symptoms include fever, pain during sex and abdominal pain.

Treatment—Men diagnosed with chlamydia should tell their partners right away. Often a woman doesn't have symptoms. She learns she has chlamydia only when a sex partner tells her he is infected. When diagnosed early, chlamydia can be cured easily with antibiotics. New tests for chlamydia are becoming more widely available.

Prevention—The best way to avoid chlamydia is to know your sex partner. If either of you had sex with anyone else, use precautions, especially condoms, and have regular medical checkups. A pregnant woman should be especially cautious because untreated chlamydia can cause eye, ear, or lung infections in her baby.

HEPATITIS

Hepatitis B mainly attacks young men and women in their teens and twenties. Like herpes, once you contract hepatitis, you become a carrier for life.

Hepatitis B attacks the liver. Both hepatitis B virus (HBV) and hepatitis C (HCV) can be sexually transmitted, however, you *MUST* go way beyond normal prevention with hepatitis because it can be spread by direct contact with an infected person through open sores and cuts. If you know someone who is infected, you can contract hepatitis B by using the same glass, toothbrush, razor or using the same pierced jewelry as someone who has it. Once you have hepatitis B your chance of contracting liver cancer is much higher than normal.

Symptoms—Dark urine, unexplainable tiredness, nausea, symptoms like stomach flu or yellowing of the eyes and skin are all common symptoms. Consult your doctor right away if you experience any of these.

Treatment—The treatment for hepatitis B consists of a series of shots by a doctor, bed rest and a special diet high in protein and carbohydrates.

Prevention—Unlike other STDs, hepatitis B can be transmitted by direct contact with saliva. Therefore, you cannot kiss an infected person or come in contact with any open cuts or sores on the infected person's body. Using condoms and safe sex precautions will *NOT* prevent infection. When properly used, latex barriers and latex condoms with a spermicide will protect against infected semen and vaginal secretions, however, they will *NOT* protect you from becoming infected with hepatitis B. Hepatitis B is transmitted through direct contact with infected persons and is more infectious than other STDs.

What Should You Do
If You Have A Sexually Transmitted Disease?

If you believe you have some of the symptoms of a sexually transmitted disease remember that this is a disease that can be treated. It is not a stigma. Do no become embarrassed or worried. Early diagnosis is the key to treatment and control. The first thing to do is to see your physician. Diagnosis is the first step in the treatment and cure for most of the diseases. Be sure to tell your doctor everything—your complete sexual history and partners with whom you have been involved. Follow the medical treatment completely and take proper precautions during your treatment until your doctor says it is permissible to resume sexual activity.

Caring, lasting relationships are built not only on having fun together but also on caring about each other's well being. If you have a STD, you and your partner can work together to solve a common health problem that belongs not just to you or your partner, but to both of you. When you take the 8 steps toward treatment, you are talking steps that show you care about each other.

You Can Control Sexually Transmitted Diseases

Misinformation or really unrealistic expectations about sex contribute to the spreading of STDs. The first stage of controlling STDs is to correct his misinformation and myths about how people transmit the diseases and next to remove anxiety from sexual encounters by knowing how to practice safer sex.

The only sure ways of not contacting STDs is by abstinence from sex or having a monogamous relationship with someone that has had a complete medical exam and blood test and you know is disease free.

Cardinal Rule

First—earn about STDs.
Second—Recognize their symptoms & warning signals
Third—get proper medical treatment
Fourth—Learn how to prevent and use safe sex

Leading Cause of Infertility

Although PID (Pelvic Inflammatory disease) is not listed as a sexually transmitted disease, it is the leading cause of infertility and affects more than one million women each year. More than 100,000 women each year become infertile as a result of PID, and a great many of the ectopic or tubal pregnancies are due to PID.

PID is a pelvic inflammatory disease (PID), an infection of the upper genital tract that can spread to the uterus, ovaries, fallopian tubes, or other related structures, often resulting in future infertility.

PID is marked by lower abdominal pain and abnormal vaginal discharge. Other symptoms may include fever, pain in the right upper abdomen. Fever, flu like symptoms, painful intercourse and irregular menstrual bleeding, however, the symptoms may be so minor that you are not aware of the illness and left untreated can seriously damage the reproductive organs.

Condoms will reduce the risk of PID (according to study at the University of Pittsburgh Medical Center). In fact inconsistent use of condoms or not using them 100% of the time actually doubled the risk of PID.

When used correctly and consistently, male latex condoms will prevent transmission of gonorrhea and partially protect against chlamydia infection.

Inconsistent use of barrier methods of contraception, particularly condoms, is really harmful. If you are going to use barrier methods, you better make sure that you are using them correctly and consistently.

Quick Reference Chart For Most Common STDs.

Any of these STDs can be transmitted through sexual contact (including vaginal and anal intercourse or oral sex) with an infected partner who may or may not have symptoms.

	What are the signs?	How is it treated?	Possible problems
Chlamydia	Men: Burning on urination and discharge from the penis. Women: Often no symptoms until PID begins. People often have no symptoms but are still infected and able to transmit chlamydia.	Infected persons and their sexual partners must be tested and/or treated with antibiotics. Curable.	PID and infertility in women, including an increased risk of ectopic (tubal) pregnancy. In men, infection of the prostate and epididymis.
Human Papillomavirus Infection (HPV) (including genital warts, Condylomas)	Warts appear as painless growths around the genitals in men and women. Potentially pre-cancerous cell changes and some types of warts are not visible to the naked eye. People who are infected but who don't have symptoms can still transmit the virus	For warts: cryotherapy, laser, or chemical treatment. For cervical changes: cryotherapy or laser. Women must have regular, follow pap smears to check for recurrences.	Some cell changes, especially the cervix, can be pre-cancerous. Recurrences are possible.
Herpes	Sores around mouth (cold sores), genital or anus, often with small painful blisters. Sores may be hidden or overlooked. Oral-genital sex when your partner has a cold sore will cause genital herpes. Some people also have flu like symptoms. Some people have no symptoms but are still infected and able to transmit the virus.	Infected persons should avoid anal, oral, and vaginal intercourse while sores persist. Acyclovir capsules or ointment may be helpful but will not cure herpes. Repeat outbreaks are common but occur at very variable intervals. Treatable but not curable.	May contribute to cervical cancer and problems in newborn babies.

Hepatitis B	Fatigue, nausea, and jaundice with dark urine; some people, however, experience no symptoms, or only mild ones.	Diagnosis requires lab tests. Treatment directed at relieving symptoms and maintaining nutrition. Completely preventative by hepatitis B vaccine.	Some people become chronic hepatitis B carriers, whether or not they continue to show symptoms of hepatitis B infection. In some cases, scarring of the liver, liver cancer, or, really death may occur.
Gonorrhea	Men: burning on urination and discharge from penis; sometimes sore throat or diarrhea. Women: often no symptoms until PID begins. Some people have no symptoms but are still infected and able to transmit the gonorrhea bacteria, especially when gonorrhea occurs in the throat or rectum.	Infected persons and their sexual partners must be tested and treated with antibiotics. Curable.	In women, PID and fertility problems, including an increased risk of ectopic (tubal) pregnancy. In men, infection of the prostate or epididymis. In both, injection of the joints, skin, and bloodstream.
Syphilis	Painless ulcer (chancre) at point of contact, usually penile shaft, around vaginal opening, or anus. Secondary stage may include a rash, swollen lymph nodes.	Infected persons and their sexual partners must be tested and treated with antibiotics. Curable without long-term consequences only if treated early.	If untreated, may affect brain, heart, pregnancies, or even be fatal.
Human Immunodeficiency Virus (HIV) Infection/AIDS (Acquired Immune Deficiency Syndrome)	Most people infected with HIV may show no symptoms for many years but are still able to transmit HIV. See ACHA's pamphlet, "HIV Infection AIDS: What Everyone Should Know," for more information.	New medications may slow down the course of HIV infection and prevent many complications. If you are concerned, consult an experienced health care provider or counselor about HIV antibody testing and appropriate medical evaluations.	HIV causes a spectrum of conditions from mild symptoms to a severe immune deficiency state (AIDS); people with AIDS experience unusual, life-threatening infections, cancers, and neurological problems.

▼

CHAPTER XIII

THE MALE SEXUAL ANATOMY

The male and female sex organs (genitals) are in a constant state of development and change from the time of birth until our death. The sex organs are also the reproductive organs of the body. When a man and woman have sexual intercourse and the man has an orgasm, sperm comes through his penis into the woman's vagina. If the sperm comes in contact with an egg in the uterus, then the woman can conceive and become pregnant (sperm can leak out of the penis and into the vagina without a man having an orgasm). The reproductive system of both the male and female are very simple in design, yet very complex in how they function. It is the same reproductive system that creates the pleasure and gratification of a sexual relationship.

The male's sex organs (genitals) are the penis and the scrotum. The testicles, two separate oval shaped eggs that produce sperm, are located inside the scrotum. Males produce sperm in their testicles. When a male becomes aroused and sexually excited, the penis will become erect and very hard. When a man obtains his ejaculation or climax, it is called an orgasm.

The cone-shaped part of the penis, the glans, is very sensitive, as well as the back-side of the shaft of the penis.

The sexual Anatomy of a male Consists of:

Penis:	This organ is outside the male body. It is the organ that a man urinates with. It is also the sexual organ that during intercourse penetrates the females vagina. The end of the penis is usually cone-shaped and is referred to as the glans.
Testicles:	These are two separate oval-shaped eggs (balls) that produce sperm.
Scrotum:	The container or pouch of skin that holds the testicles and allows the sperm to be produced.
Vas Deferens:	This tube-like part enables the sperm to move from the epididymis and through the urethra to the ampulla.
Ampulla:	The enlarged end of the vas deferens. The ampulla is the staging area where the semen is made up from different body fluids along with the sperm.
Prostate:	The prostate is a gland that surrounds the neck of the bladder and the urethra. The function of the prostate gland is to produce a thin milky fluid that also mixes with sperm to help protect them during their travels.
Seminal Vesicle:	A mucus-like fluid is produced by this bag-like structure. This fluid then mixes with sperm and helps keep the sperm healthy.
Cowper's Glands:	Consists of two small round glands below the prostate gland. The purpose of these glands is to produce a mucous-like fluid that lubricates the end of the penis

	before intercourse and to help the transport and protection of the sperm.
Urethra:	The urethra extends from the bladder to the opening at the tip of the penis. This tube is what carries the urine or semen to the outside of the body.
Urinary Opening:	Refers to the end of the penis and the slit or opening that urine and semen come out of.
Sperm:	A sperm (spermatozoa) is a tiny egg that looks like a tadpole. It is this cell that joins with the female's egg to create a baby.
Semen:	During sexual intercourse, a fluid is ejected from the urinary opening. The semen fluid is made up of seminal vaginal fluid, prostate gland fluid, a small amount of Cowper's Gland fluid and sperm. During intercourse, it is the job of the semen to work it's way into a woman's uterus to come in contact with the woman's egg produced by the ovaries.
Erection:	The process where the penis changes from flaccid (soft) to engorge itself with blood and become hard and erect.
Ejaculation:	The process when semen comes out of the urinary opening of the penis.
Foreskin:	Refers to the area of loose skin around the glans penis and the upper shaft of the penis. If a male is not circumcised, foreskin will refer to the cover of skin over the glans penis.

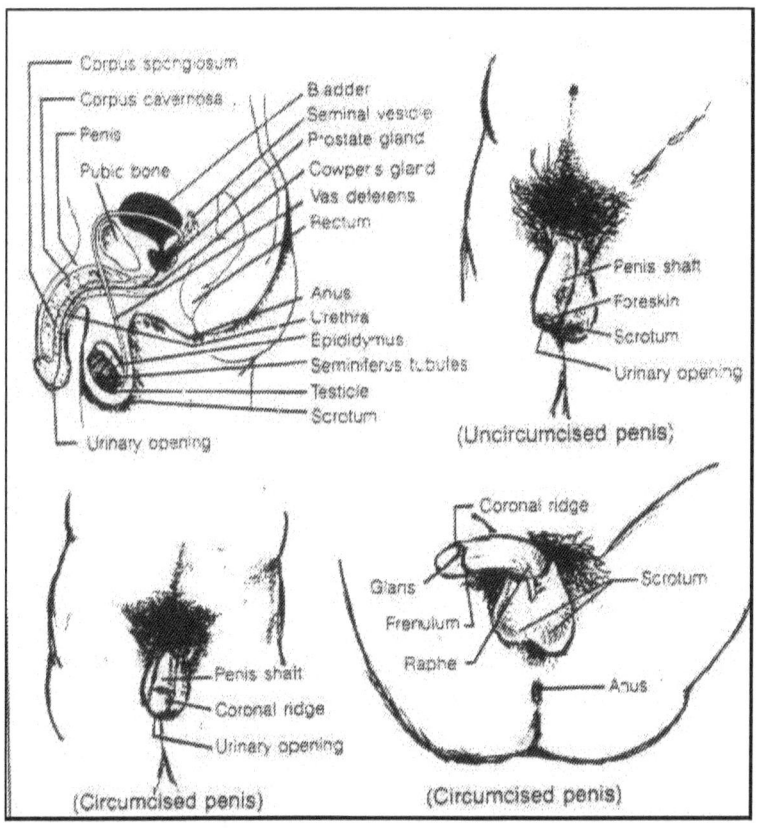

Male sex and reproductive system

The function of the penis is thought to be understood by most. However, "there is no organ about which more misinformation has been perpetuated," William Master, M.D., and Virginia Johnson of the Masters and Johnson Institute in Virginia once observed. "That amazing item of flesh has been venerated in cults, reviled and misrepresented in folk legends and mutilated, decorated, hidden, exposed, adorned and feared throughout the centuries. It is the item that is on every young man's mind as he grows up. It is the item that gives a great deal of frustration and anxiety because people are not sure how it should look, how it should perform, how they should treat it and how to properly use it."

Cardinal Rule

Young men are caught up in the false big penis mythology and are always worried about how they measure up to others. However, the truth is that there is no correlation between penis size and sexual pleasure.

In truth, the reproductive cycle for the male is very simple. The male has two testicles. They are shaped like small eggs and held in the scrotum, a pouch of skin outside of the body. The purpose of the testicles is to produce the male eggs or cells which are called sperm. During intercourse, the sperm produced can enter into the female and fertilize the female's egg , eventually producing an embryo.

The process is initiated when the male becomes sexually aroused and excited. The male sperm that is produced in the testicles and has moved to the epididymis so that the sperm can grow and mature will leave the epididymis via the vas deferens and travel to the ampulla where it is combined with other fluids to create the semen. While this is happening, the Cowper's glands have produced a fluid to coat the urethra and protect the sperm as it travels through the penis. At this point, there is a great deal of pelvic thrusting and ejaculation whereby the semen is pushed through the urinary opening. The rhythmic contractions of the muscles near the base of the penis drive the semen to go like spurts. The actual amount of volume during ejaculation varies from man to man. It also tends to decrease with age and increase with the length of time between ejaculations. Ejaculation usually produces a tremendous sensation of release because after it occurs, there is a release of the muscle tension and a gradual relaxation of the penis. After an ejaculation, the man will then return to what is known as the refractory period between ejaculations. This term refers to the time that is necessary for the body to rest and recuperate before the male can perform an erection and orgasm again. The refractory period usually gets longer as you get older. However, the periods vary from man to man and the more frequently a man ejaculates, the shorter the in between period it is likely to be. However, the average male will only have an ejaculation orgasm once a day in a 24 hour cycle.

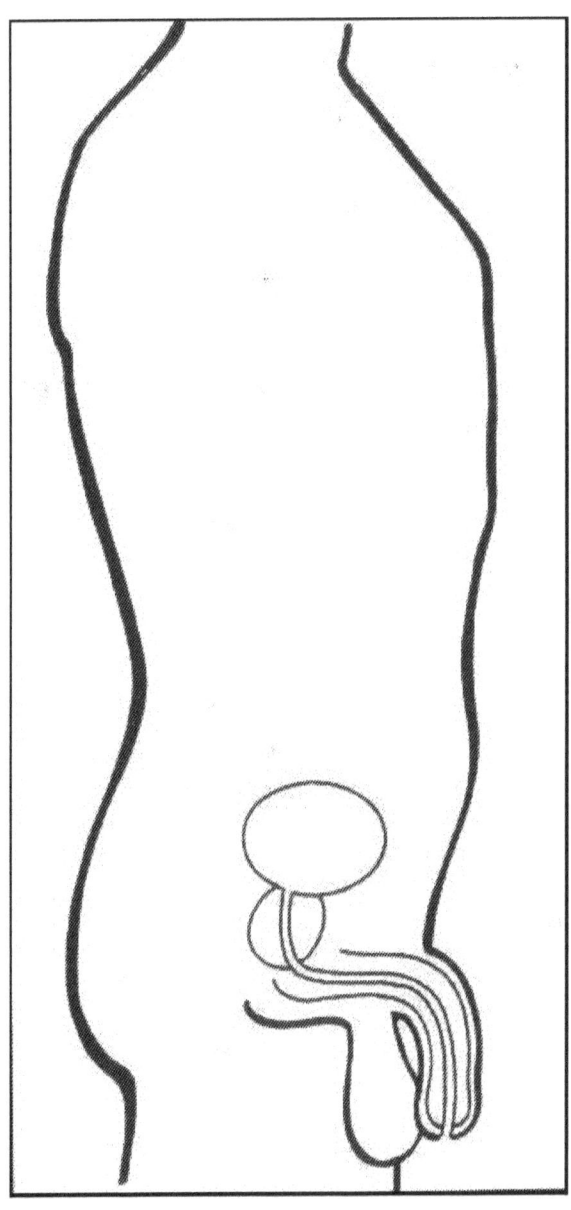

CHAPTER XIV

▼

THE FEMALE SEXUAL ANATOMY

The female sexual organs are both inside and outside of the body and are more complex and thus there is frequently confusion or misunderstanding by both men and women regarding the female organs.

A woman should get a more accurate picture of her body. It is smart to know and understand how the body works and functions. If you have not had the opportunity before, take the time to give yourself a self- examination and explore the genital area.

The sexual area between a woman's legs is called the genital area or vulva. The woman has folds of flesh called lips in the genital area. The large outer lips are referred to as the labia majora or simply as the labia. Inside that is the labia minora, the small inner lips that protect the vagina opening. At the top of the small lips is a little bud referred to as the clitoris. The clitoris is extremely sensitive and when stimulated gives a woman sexual pleasure. When a woman is aroused, the blood vessels in the genital area and inner lips swell and her clitoris becomes erect. During an orgasm women will have a series of muscle contractions leading to an eventual release of tension.

The organs inside the woman are the vagina, uterus, fallopian tubes and ovaries.

THE FEMALE ANATOMY:

Vulva or genital area:	That part of the external part of the female anatomy between her legs.
Mons veneris:	The layer of fatty tissue that pads the pelvic bone underneath it. It is usually covered with hair.
Clitoral Hood:	The clitoral hood may cover all of the clitoris or just a section. It is a layer of skin.
Clitoris:	This is a very sensitive organ responsible for generating sexual excitement in a woman. It is very small, and when it is touched or aroused it will become enlarged with blood much like a man's penis and become erect.
Vaginal Opening:	The vaginal opening refers to the area where the female's menstrual flow during her period flows out. It is also the opening where a erect penis penetrates during the act of intercourse.
Urethra Opening:	The female urethra urinates from this opening.
Hymen:	Refers to a piece of skin that is either partially or totally covers the vagina opening. It is believed that this delicate membrane can tell whether a person is a virgin or not. In reality, the hymen can become torn during any number of activities, including exercise and masturbation. Even doctors cannot tell for sure if a female has had sex. However, it is kind of a folklore that if the hymen is in place that a woman is still a virgin. However, medical reports have shown that because the hymen may be stronger in certain females, that even pregnant females can still have a hymen intact.
Labia Minora:	Refers to the small inner lips that protect the vagina opening.

Labia Majora: Refers to the large outer lips that protect the vagina area.

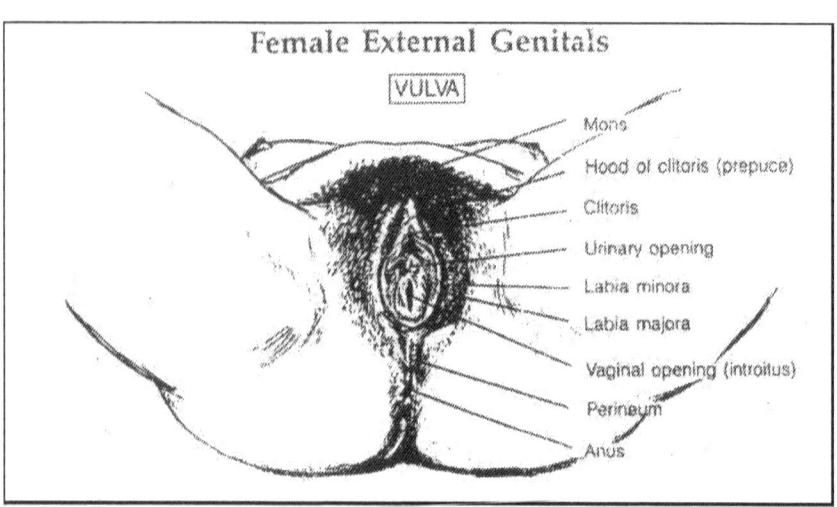

Female External Genitals

Ovarian Follicles: Refers to the compartments that make up the ovaries and that hold the individual ovum until it is ripe and ready to be released.

Ovaries: Refers to the two oval shaped structures that holds the female eggs.

Ovum: Refers to the tiny eggs that carries the mother's genetic matrix and that becomes fertilized during intercourse by the male's sperm.

Fallopian Tubes: Refers to the fragile thin tubes that carry the ova to the uterus.

Uterus: A pear shaped hollow muscular organ where the fetus will develop. It is this area that becomes blood enriched during the menstrual cycle and then sheds the enriched tissue during menstruation.

Fimbria: Refers to the small finger-like extensions at the end of the fallopian tubes.

Cervix: This a small opening between the uterus and the vagina. It separates the vagina from the uterus.

Bartholin's Glands: Refers to the two small glands that are located inside the walls of the vagina and that have the capability to secrete fluid.

Endometrium: This refers to the layer of skin on the uterus that gets thick and falls off during menstruation.

Vagina: Refers to the hollow passage way that connects the uterus to the outside of the body and at the vagina opening is the area where the small inner lips, large inner lips and the clitoris are located.

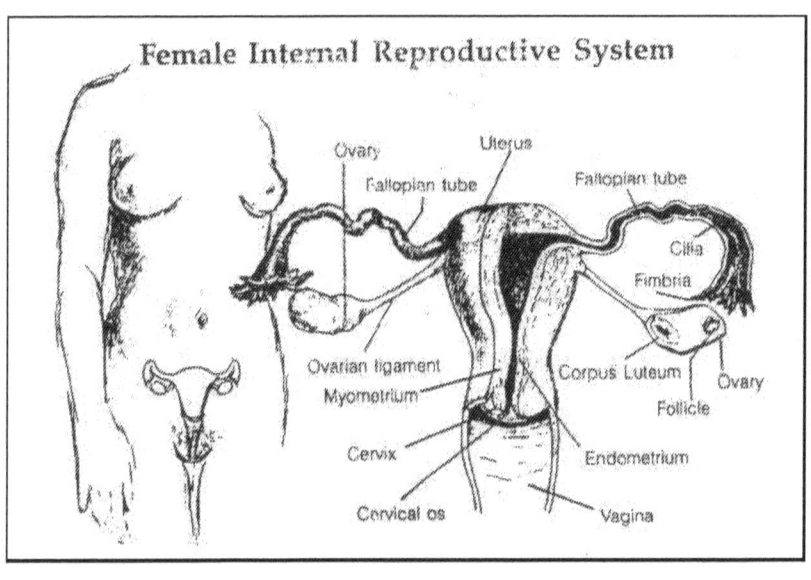

Female Internal Reproductive System

Reproductive System

Women in today's society have much more control over their reproductive lives than they ever have before historically. To a certain extent that means that women can plan when to have children. This is a very important fact that can affect a relationship in a positive way. This enables the father to be an active partner in planning and raising the child. This also enables the woman to wait until she finds the right partner so she has both a good husband and father. If your relationship has a good foundation, then having a child together is both an expression of love and a strong bond.

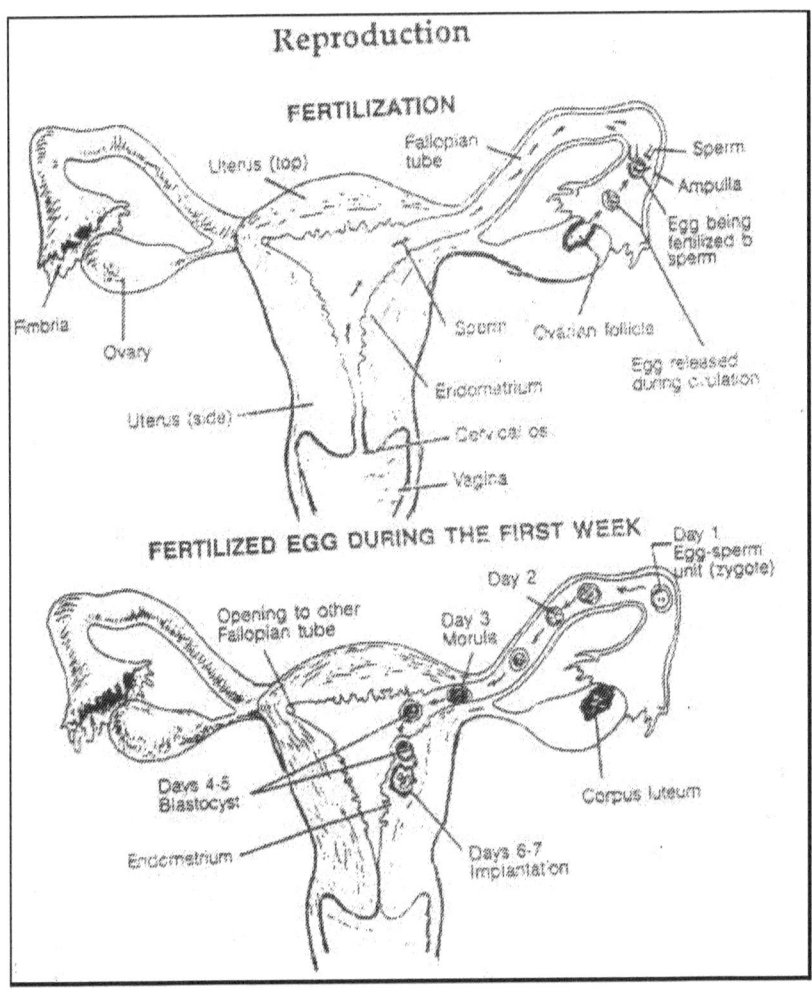

The Breasts

The pair of mammae occurring on the chest usually starts to develop sometime after the age of 12 in a female. This is also the signal that puberty has started. In every culture throughout history more has been written about the anatomy of a woman's breasts than any other feature. It seems to hold a special place in almost any culture and is even associated with fertility in many cultures. The breast may change in shape and size during the evolvement of the female. The female breast is an important part of the reproductive system because it is made up of numerous milk glands, sometimes called mammary glands. These glands are surrounded by protective fatty tissue. Each breast has a larger darkened area called the areola. This area is very sensitive to both touch and temperature. That is why when it is very cold sometimes the woman's breasts will become very taunt and perky. It is also the area that during sexual gratification will become tender and sensitive and responsive with physical changes. Towards the center of the areola is a round nipple. This is a slight protrusion from the woman's tip of the breast and it is where the milk ducts discharge. The milk ducts are inside the breast itself and come up against the chest wall.

A woman's breasts undergo numerous changes during sexual arousal and can be the source of much pleasure and gratification. The nipple erection is usually a sign of sexual arousal and then the areolas will swell because they are becoming engorged with blood. This also makes the nipples and breasts more sensitive to touch.

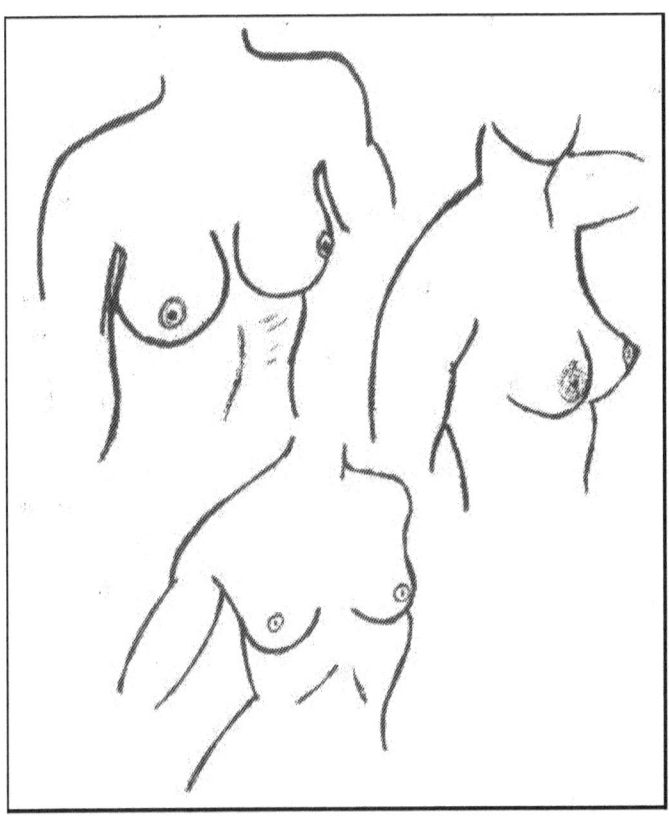

▼

BEYOND SAFE SEX

By providing you with the following information and knowledge on safe sex and birth control, I hope you will fee secure and capable of taking control of your sexual activity and able to enjoy the pleasures of a good sexual relationship.

Birth control refers to many different methods that are employed to prevent unwanted pregnancies. However, birth control devices, technique and methods should never be confused with safe sex procedures because most birth control methods offer little or no protection regarding sexually transmitted diseases.

There are numerous birth control methods that are improper and non-effective. It is unfortunate because of the veil of secrecy that all too many people have been shocked when they found out that the woman was pregnant because they were under the false belief that they were practicing some form of birth control. All birth control devices either destroy or prevent the live sperm from performing its mission to fertilize the female egg. The average sperm has a life span of approximately 72 hours although some can live longer. The egg usually has a lifespan of approximately 24 hours during each monthly cycle. However, sperm stubbornly resist any effort to stop their progress and once the sperm reaches the cervix and starts its migration upward towards the fallopian tubes it may be there several days waiting for the egg. That is why many times people using different birth control methods are caught off guard.

The following are poor means of birth control:

The rhythm method depends on the people precisely knowing when ovulation takes place and avoiding having intercourse during this time. In theory it sounds fine. In actual practice many times it does not work because it is extremely difficult to predict with accuracy when ovulation is taking place.

Coitalus interruptus refers to the technique of withdrawing the penis from the vagina before the male ejaculation. This might seem a good technique, however, it is quite ineffective. Although this method requires no equipment or medication, it does not work very well for a variety of reasons. First, it requires the man to withdraw at the moment of greatest passion. It puts all the responsibility on the man but the consequences on the woman. Most importantly, in many cases, during sexual arousement, long before ejaculation occurs, tiny droplets of clear fluid filled with sperm escape from the tip of the penis. It takes only one sperm to cause conception.

Female condoms are devices that are more expensive than male condoms. They have a greater tendency to be pushed aside or slip during intercourse and are not as reliable as the male condom.

IUDs (Intra Uterine Devices IUD was effective as a birth control, 1% of the times when women did get pregnant there was a much higher chance the pregnancy would be ectopic (a pregnancy where the baby grows outside the uterus, usually in the fallopian tube). The major advantage of the IUD is it is a long- term birth control method and is very effective.) and in theory are great. A doctor must insert a small plastic apparatus into the uterus. As long as it remains in place, it will prevent pregnancies. However, in real life it turned out that the IUDs had many side effects. They had a tendency to cause bad pelvic infections. They were, at times, causing pain and undue cramping in the women.

Various Birth Control Methods

Today women have a wide variety of birth control options. The Norplant implant is a long-range and expensive method. There are female diaphragms, the cervical cap, the female sponge, numerous spermicides, jellies and creams designed to kill or immobilize sperm and are readily available. There's even a morning after pill when all else has failed or been forgotten. The morning after pill requires a prescription and a visit to the doctor's office.

Sterilization is the ultimate birth control. Either the male or female is sterilized. This can be accomplished in one of two ways, either by a surgical procedure performed by a qualified physician or through the use of certain drugs.

Oral contraceptives work and are effective as long as the woman remembers to take the pill. The chemical in the pill simply fools the woman's body into believing that she is pregnant so the ovaries will not release any eggs into the fallopian tubes. The hormones that are produced by the pituitary gland at the base of the brain control the growth of a few eggs each month and the production of the female sex hormone estrogen by the ovary. This process is fairly dependable, however, some women do have side effects from the use of the pill. Although there are many versions of the pill they still function in pretty much the same way. The pill can also be expensive in comparison to other forms of birth control. Since the pill relies upon the use of drugs in some cases the side effects can be severe and in a few cases it has been known to increase the risk of cancer in the ovaries. There are new formulas and pills coming on the market that have been tested and proclaim that they have eliminated the bad side effects. However, the choice of the pill should be left up to the woman and her physician if it is appropriate and effective.

The latex condom is perhaps the easiest, most reliable and effective form of birth control if used properly with a spermicide. The medical statistics show that latex condoms are about 97% effective in preventing pregnancy. In addition, unlike all of the other previously mentioned methods or devices of birth control, it has one major advantage. It is an effective protection or defense against sexually transmitted diseases as well as unwanted pregnancies. Also, the condom is easily obtainable and transportable. This makes the condom the all around most versatile and effective form of safe sex and birth control.

Personal hygiene and personal exam

This section would not be complete without a discussion on personal hygiene and personal examination. Each of us should be responsible for doing self examinations regularly while bathing and notice any changes or symptoms in our bodies. This is very important for everyone, not just sexually active people.

Just below the vaginal opening and where the labia meet is a small area of smooth, usually hairless, skin. Below that is the anus (this opening is the area where fecal matter passes from the bowels). Women should always be careful to wipe from the front to the back after using the toilet to avoid having fecal matter transferred near the vaginal and urinary openings. This can be a common cause of vaginal and uterine infections.

Female Sexual Hygiene

Women, because of their special internal reproductive anatomy should pay special attention to their menstrual cycle. Physicians recommend that from the age of puberty you should keep a record of when you have your menstrual cycle. It can be invaluable for diagnosing many different types of problems and is much more accurate then vague recollections when you are talking to a doctor about changes in your cycle. The average length between one menstrual flow and the next is 28 days. However, cycle lengths vary from one woman to another. As a woman goes from puberty to menopause she can have tremendous variations in her cycle and amount of menstrual flow. Sometimes while a woman is maturing the periods may vary in timing, amount and color. All of this can be natural and should not be alarming. However, it is important to be aware of your menstrual cycle when you are discussing problems with your physician. The changes may be symptoms of something that needs treatment.

The female external genitals should be periodically examined. If any change takes place, you should contact your physician immediately. Just below the clitoris is a very small urinary opening. Below that is the vaginal opening. Because these openings are so close to each other, many women experience urinary infections after having sex. Women should understand their anatomy and learn to recognize signs of problems early, especially during the reproductive cycle.

Male Sexual Hygiene

A recommended routine for a man while in the shower is a self exam on his penis and testicles to see if there are any unusual marks, lumps, or coloring of the skin. If any change takes place, you should contact your doctor immediately.

Every man and woman must take responsibility for monitoring their own health and also be aware of the symptoms of sexually transmitted diseases. Always schedule a medical examination whenever changes or symptoms of a problem are noticed. Sexually active people should be checked twice a year for STDs and sexually active women should have a yearly pelvic exam and pap smear.

Unfortunately, many parents think that because teens look fine and are young adults, that regular check ups are no longer necessary. However, teens do need to have regular exams so that doctors can follow their growth and physical development and screen for changes that signal that something is not right or for disorders or substance abuse. It can be a great comfort to a teen if they have an established relationship with a doctor because it is very difficult for a teen to talk about sex, STDs and the private parts of their body. Embarrassment, fear or guilt cause a lot of teens to go untreated when they become infected with a STD. That is why even though the cure is available many go untreated and put a whole generation of teens at risk. It is estimated that 1 out of every 6 teens will contract an STD disease. Because most teenagers are very afraid of how their parents will react, they will go untreated.

In order to create a solid relationship between parent and teen and between two partners, you must have a free flow of communication. You may have empathy for the other person, however, we all know that it does no good to say to a loved one after the fact, "If I had only known."

Stay Healthy

Keep yourself physically fit and sexually active and you can go on enjoying satisfying and pleasurable sex almost to the very end of your life. A 72-year old woman told researchers Bernard Starr, Ph.D., and Marcella Weintar, Ph.D., "Our sex is so much more relaxed I know my body better, and we know each other better. Sex is unhurried and the *best* in our lives."

Tips to stay healthy*

- Eat a balanced diet
- Get plenty of rest
- Exercise regularly
- Avoid infections
- Learn to relax and deal with stress

- Do not take unnecessary medications—especially antibiotics and steroids
- Practice safe sex
- Do not use drugs like marijuana, speed, cocaine, downers, nicotine or heroin

*Department of Health and Human Services.

Cardinal Rule

A healthy body increases the pleasure of sex, sexual activity, can rejuvenate the body, and you alone have control over one of the greatest ways to pleasure yourself. Use this control wisely and prudently

ABOUT THE AUTHOR

▼

Author Background

Rescue 911 Series Foundation
P.O. Box 511
Troy, Michigan 48099
Free information brochure: 877-473-9435
Phone line 877-4SEX HELP

Ronald A. Hagen is a highly motivated, investigative researcher with over 12 years of experience compiling information regarding sex, love and relationships.

Mr. Hagen was trained as an analyst and researcher while he was an agent with the Central Intelligence Agency. He has adapted this skill to the field of love and relationships, and has spent thousand of hours reviewing facts and theories about relationships. He has exhaustively examined hundreds of exit interviews of couples, has been involved with numerous support groups, and has corresponded with both the federal and state health departments on STDs and relationships. As a result of these experiences, Hagen has been exposed to virtually every theory regarding relationships.

Additionally, Mr. Hagen has worked with several school organizations in developing programs for teens. He is cochairman of the STDs foundation and has worked with the Michigan State Health Department to co-produce television programs for channel 62 regarding teen dating and safe sex. He has written brochures and pamphlets regarding safe sex and abstinence and was featured on cable TV in a half-hour program dealing with communication and components for developing a successful relationship. He has appeared on the radio station WNZK for the program Bright Side of Aging in discussions regarding seniors and their evolving relationships.

Mr. Hagen has conducted seminars and lectures for numerous community organizations. He is the author of What You Always Wanted to Know About Sexually Transmitted Diseases, "The New Teen Dating Game, and Love, Sex and Relationships Where Would We Be Without Them. Hagen teaches courses at Macomb Community College regarding relationships and teen dating.

0-595-20994-7